Plat ove

Compiled by Irtiqa Noor Ansari

Td
HOME OF VENTURES

Published By

True Dreamster

ISBN: 978-93-91887-28-5

About True Dreamster

Established on 23rd July 2017, True Dreamster is one among the fastest growing self-publishing companies in the country, with over 500+ published books and 3000+ newly launched authors under our belt. Our pivotal objective is to transform the dreams of all literary enthusiasts into actuality, and we strive to grow bigger and better, launching umpteenth number of writers in the further coming years.

We have been operating successfully as an evolving community of writers and literature enthusiasts; have organized multiple sensational events in different cities across India.

We have a crew of committed and talented young members who are the best at what they do and work together ardently to bring all the services under one roof just for you. Our quality is our strength and we treasure gratified customers more than anything else.

Follow us:

@true_dreamster

publishing@truedreamster.com

www.truedreamster.com

Contents

Irtiqa Noor Ansari

Irtiqa Noor Ansari lives in Kanpur U.P India is a college student. An ambitious dreamer; Irtiqa loves Calligraphy, Drawing, painting, and other arts too. She recently started writing poems. She is a fan of Korean drama and likes to read webtoons. Irtiqa loves nature; she often travels to admire nature's beauty. Platonic - eternal love is her first anthology as a compiler. You can get in touch with her on Instagram @irti.noor

A Friend

A friend who guides you like Father,

A friend who loves you like Mother,

A friend who teases you like a Brother,

A friend who comforts you like a Sister,

A friend who showers you with Love,

A friend who makes you feel Safe,

A friend who enjoys with you in your Best,

A friend who stays with you in your Worst,

A friend who accepts your Past,

A friend who supports your Present,

A friend who motivates you for the Future,

A friend who values your Worth,

A friend who hangs out with you on Weekends,

A friend who helps you in Study,

A friend who encourages you to do your best in everything,

Never lose that precious human being,

It's so hard to find a true friend,

The world is full of fake friends,

If you have a best friend,

Don't lose them till the end.

Color Blind

How many colors are there?

Red, green, yellow, orange, purple.

There are bright and dull colors,

Vibrant and boring colors.

I heard plants, trees, leaves are green,

There are different shades of color to be seen,

I heard sky, sea, oceans are blue,

Some colors are dark and some colors are hue.

I heard the sun looks reddish-yellow,

I think of it when I lay on the pillow.

I heard the moon looks beautiful at night,

Stars look like a diamond as they shine bright.

I heard flowers hold different colors,

Rose, Lotus, Daisy, Lilly, Trumpet creeper.

I heard Cherry, Strawberry, Apples are red,

The sky also turns red when the sunset.

The beautiful colorful world must be so pretty,

I could only imagine all the amazing beauty.

As for me, the world seems Black and White,

I couldn't see all those brilliant colors since I am COLOR BLIND.

But I can feel those colors with my closed eyes,

I can feel the beauty of those mesmerizing colorful sites.

I maybe disable with my eyes,

But I believe that one day, on my own I'll rise.

Memories

Memories are made and are meant to stay.

But I just want mine to just go away,

I don't need memories to remind me of the past,

All i need is for them to be erased really fast.

Each memory takes up space in my mind,

Where is an off switch that I desperately wanna find??

I don't mind not having anything in my head,

Because memories are the most thing that I dread.

Memories are your enemies they ruin your life,

It’s like being stabbed with a poisoned

Knife.

You'll always have that memory where ever you go,

I tried to forget it all but nothing worked

Though.

It's going to take time, maybe evens years

Memories will never help you wipe your tears

They'll just only make your tears keep rolling down,

And you'll be left with that ugly frown.

Memories will choose to stay or leave as they wish,

They'll swim out of your mind like a slippery little fish.

They might evens stay for the longest time,

And trying to get away from them

Will be a very high climb.

Memories can be a blessing or a curse

But mine be remaining like a curse.

Aaron Blackie

He is Aaron Blackie, a citizen of Nigeria. He is a Poet, Novelist and a Blogger. He lives with his family in Warri Delta State-Nigeria

Change- The Measure of the Sea!

The cry for change...
All are clamoring for change
The deeper the well, the purer the water:
Change is
The measure of the sister in you
The measure of the brother in you
What you get is what you are...

What you get is what you are
Lest, the ram would have wished
To be the knife
The knife would have wish
To be the busher:
All on to man, man on to none...

What you get is what you are
Lest, the metal would have wished
To be the anvil
The anvil would have wished
To be the hammer
The hammer would have wished
To be the blacksmith:
All on to ma, man on to man...

All over the place
Love is become the sneaking
Chameleon:
Face that smiled brightly at you,

In the morning time,
Becoming the same faces, spitting venom
At you in the evening time...

Because faith is locked within the armpit
Of strange gods:
Then love lost her sweet-scent
To tasteless relationships;
Hope lost let brushes
To colourless futurity,
And vision lost her essences,
To the drifting oceans...

Thus, what you get is what you are
Lest, God in man, man in God:
Love that knows no boundary, nor race
Nor colour:
Boundless, selfless, sacrificial and
Eternal- Christ love

Look, sister, brother...
The deeper the well, the purer the water:
Change is
The measure of the sister in you
The measure of the brother in you
What you get, is what you are...
So let take it deeper

We are what we are.

We are what we are:
Creatures
Created to feeling and
Slavish
Unto our emotions,
Cleaving
Unto our self-indulged passions-
Zeal's over much,
That flow like surging river
Beyond its bank...

We are what we are:
Man
Born of a woman
Of his own bones
Alas!
Companionship is made
One and whole
Yet are there no eyes-
Are there
No eyes roving restlessly before
Variegated fleshes
Like chameleons without their
Own dresses?
Then beauty
Cannot look each other's face
Beyond tomorrow
For beauty is as truth as trust as
Respect as honesty..

O what a sweet thought robed
With the Rope of loophole wisdom!

We are what we are:
Man
Conceived out of His own
Love;
Out of His own purifying
Likeness;
Out of His graceful and glorious
Image;
Out of His own in-depth compassion
And comely identity
Thus we are what Christ left us:
Sons of
Men unto Sons of God
Refined,
To love to be crucified and died
For being
The lovers we are and for the heavenly ways

Adiel Holster

Hello everyone.

I am Adiel Holster; I was born on October 4 2001. I'm a Muslim, and I do my religious studies and poetry in my free time. I am the last born of 7 children.
I hate violence and I love peace. Thank you all, please accept.

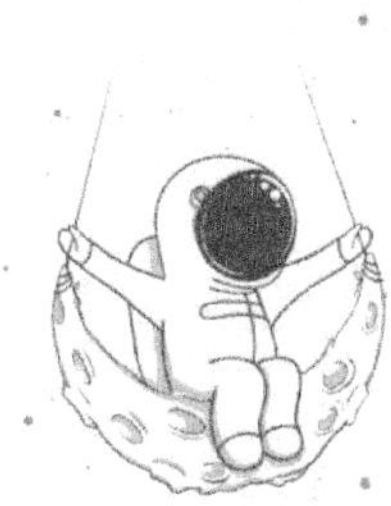

Eternal Love

Eternal Love is a feeling
That lives in heart;
I don't know what I'd do
If it's broken apart.

Love is me and I am Love
A sweet and gentle dove;
A warming glove
From the Almighty above.

I try my utmost best
To finish my love quest;
This is indeed a test
I will definitely not rest.

Love is an eternal flame
In my eyes, it's the same;
I am ready for any blame
Love is my game.

This is my dream
For I'm a gentle dove;
Please support me and all
In our:Eternal Love!!

Amna Ali Syed

An MBA graduate from the heart of Islamabad, Amna has been writing poetry for more than 10 years now. She enjoys baking in her spare time and her favourite person in the world is her 3-year-old niece, Rozha!

Strangers

What's stopping me from going insane?
She asks rather curiously,
Is it the strained smile I put up?
Or the façade that has become my existence?

Staring at the blank ceiling at a distance
I'm good at pretending, she tells him
His peculiar eyes tell her he's doubtful,
As if he can see through all the lies

Oh but how do I prove it to you, friend?
I had once a stranger tell me otherwise
He said, the brightest smiles are always in hiding
So creature, what secret do you hide in those sad
eyes?

These eyes, though sad they may be
Twinkle a little, just the tiniest sparkle
The shadows surrounding them tell stories of
struggle
They are worn out but fine, just fine

The hands they grasp are soft and fragile,
They exude innocence if held close
Although the softest touch, they
shiver just a little
It's the weakness, the stranger
proclaimed

They have been cut too many times

She wonders how he knows her so well,
When often her own do not
Is it that apparent,
The glistening beneath her eyes?
All he sees are tears, instead of happiness and bright smiles.

Celestial Escape

Floating across the silver sea
I encounter some form o' modesty
My plaque of wood slowly drifting
Here comes the edge,
Don't let me fall in

This calmness won't drown away
The noise in my head,
Screaming away
A hollow melody resounds my ears
Pulls me back, to the shadows of fear

Pleasure, pain all at once
Deepening shadows, across the sun
Come on lift me
Upwards, to the sky
Dancing specks shining far; a light

Oh carry me to this mythical land
Where anything's possible
And anything can
Dreams take flight,
What could happen?
Anything might
And anything can.

Misery in beautiful places

I found misery in beautiful places
Across shining stars and empty spaces

I found it on the brightest summer days
& among laughs of cheery children in May

I found it tucked away in my small back pocket
Concealed carefully behind my sleeves of crochet

I found it behind my everyday glee face
I found it even, during my sleepless night daze

I found it everywhere it's not supposed to be
Rejoicing among those who carry it softly, like me

Oh forlorn, let not misery's company wear you down
A heavy heart still beats to life's faint, beautiful sounds.

Anadia de Beer

Anadia de Beer

Date of birth: 03 November 1990

Country of birth: South Africa

Anadia is a full time business woman, who enjoys playing with her 3 year old and writing poetry in her free time. She started writing poems at the age of 8. Recently she started taking up her love for writing poetry a bit more seriously. She gets her inspiration from her day to day life.

To my little Boy

To my little boy
You are the source of all my joy
I am so happy I was blessed with you
And for you, there is nothing I wouldn't do

Just one look at your little smile
Can make me carry on for a while
And before my energy can deplete
You surprise me again by doing something sweet

Seeing the world through your little eyes
Grownups measure happiness by size
But you taught me again, it is the little things that count
Like a leave twirling on the ground

I sometimes wish I can freeze the time
Just to spend another hour with this boy of mine
Building memories to last
Because my boy is growing up too fast.

The Demons of the Night

No matter how good a day I had
It always ends bad
The moment I get into my bed
My demons start messing with my head

The inner fight starts as I try to push them away
But I always lose the battle, and they get to stay
And I can feel my throat pull tight
As I try to deal with the demons of the night

Heartache and pain fills every inch of me
Darkness creeping in, no light to see
Tearing my soul into millions of little pieces
Sucking the life out of me like leeches

I feel the tears burning behind my eyes
Trying to convince myself, they are telling me lies
But my demons don't allow me too much time to
think
And they shut me down within a blink

And as the sun starts to come out
They wonder of and go about
Leaving me alone in the light of day
Tonight the will be back, ready to play.

A New Road

Once again I find myself at the beginning of a new road
Unable to identify, is he a frog or a toad
Scared to go in for the kiss, that might give me my prince
Going numb, can't feel my limbs

Praying for a sign
Something to confirm he will be mine
Someone to love for the rest of my life
The one, who will make me his wife

Time is the only thing that will tell
If this will be a journey to heaven or hell
With small baby steps, I will start
Opening up my heart

Not knowing what the days ahead may hold
Hopefully magical stories to be told
Of a love so pure and true
Between us two

So from today
I will give my best to play
The wonderful game of love
Maybe he was sent from up above.

Teary Eyes

The start of me and you
It was perfect, almost too good to be true
You were everything I ever wanted
But now my heart is haunted

You said everything a broken women needed to hear
Telling me, with you there is no need to fear
I can let my walls down and embrace your love
That I was sent to you from up above

What a stupid move for me to do
Bringing my walls down, letting you through
It didn't take long for the abuse to begin
Harsh, hurtful words and bruises on my skin

Your actions didn't match you words
Empty promises, just for the birds
You broke me down piece by piece
And you did it all with ease

I'm trying to keep my teary eyes dry
I'm sealing of my walls, building them high
Fading away with sorrow in my heart
Never again will I let down my guard.

Aniruddha Bhattacharya

Pandit. Aniruddha Bhattacharya is one of the most accomplished vocalists of the Kirana Gharana of Hindustani Classical music. He has been performing extensively across India and overseas including the USA, UK, and France. Born in 1971 a young Aniruddha loved music enough to start listening, appreciating, and learning very early under the able guidance of his mother Smt. Gouri Bhattacharya.Bhattacharya. is also a natural poet and composer adept in both Indian as well as Western classical. He also has two Bengali poetry books to his credit which were released in the prestigious Kolkata International Book Fair.

The Wait...

I started counting the days
From the tenth of January –
So as to get a grasp
of things –
to get over the immeasurable
heaves – between the
simple , gleeful faith
and conscious divergence –
from the haze to a
gleaming phase –
a revelation maybe –
I waited still- and
Gave myself more
of the waning moments –
to have felt
as if , the inglorious reckoning
of the violet rose-
She came still – to name All-
Subtlety .

Disarrayed

Days elapsed , enamoured of her,
As I was –
And took to a recluse corner
of the backyard bloom –
the pristine adherence of a
distant whirlwind
culminated onto a denuded
core of thoughts –
the breezing echoes of nature –
within a moment in time ,
where – come to a standstill –
the inner maneuvering of
creation has – a bizarre abstinence
as if, asking for many more
flaunting cohorts of time –
maimed as if, of something
that ends all –
As if , a lonesome herd
Yet to find the day's bounty-
Before a gruesome , shadowy dusk .
The blithe chase begins over
The sounding hedgerows.

Eternity

Still the days of roses
from an unnerving bloom
to the bleak moments of June –
seek a nadir of joy-
in perpetuation –
Alas! memories!

What is gone is gone
Through the wondrous
Cohorts of time –
Beacons of an illusory
Gleam came surfacing
From braving the variants
of unhappy moments –

yet but a raging spree
to hunt as if, an
ineffable salvation
in a dissonant stratum-
gazes the bleak corners
of the languid days .

When love breathes
An inevitable agony –
The memories and happenings
as if in a proximal cahoot
undermine the spreading anguish –
yet so real the pain can be .

Grow more – I shall,
Maybe beyond the astute agreeability
of a thronging clan-
maybe beyond a slithering
usurper's so called
overwhelming vanquish-
maybe beyond the inane
lullaby of a lonesome, nocturnal
songbird.
Ways are here –
To unfurl.

The Deranged Prisoner

So very proximal , yet
So far , that you seem to be-
as if , when the
blistering afternoon mirage
fades within the
resounding furrows of the dusk –
to gleam the summer bloom
with variants of hues-
Still but kept you far-
The inane moments have –
as the bewildered flocks
screech the evening silence
onto a bleak , dreary night .

Antonio Bernard Ma-at

He was born in 1998 in a humble city of Tanjay, Negros Oriental Philippines. Growing up, he was fascinated with arts, music and creative writing. He became a local artist as an entertainer vocalist of two resto bars in 2018-19, and currently He is a full pledge worship leader at Tanjay Assemblies of God.

Antonio is a visionary and a leader influencing the youth of AG Tanjay to live a life with divine morality as a compass. He is currently studying bachelor of business administration in marketing management, He also gain interest in mathematics, philosophy, psychology and theology. His love in poetic writing serve as his expose journal being hidden in words that expresses deep emotion and enlightenment of hope to those who read

Falling leaves

An amber seed growing on a velvet horizon
which fortress is created by the reflection of ones imagination,
kindled by the vivid sound of an eerie delusion,
that sprout a shadow of hardships forging the awareness of your souls perception.

Then a boundless pace of promethean conclusions,
with a wondering sight that makes a rational decision,
But the hasty affection of the spiral taste of nature,
can breed and postulates confidence that leads to the route of destruction.

My ticket to rest

Locked up in atrocious way
immensely drowned to voices I obey,
loops of regrets
A seven sorrow's mess,
The halo of death's threats
are ticket for me to rest.

Doodle thing

Life is a doodle thing like a gameplay of idles,
agonizing like a poetic rain , dropped as a keychain of riddles.
Begins with a bleary swords of words that pours upon the brain,
with an appetite to cease the mind of its reader.

It's a hairy knowledge whose teeth is sharper than any edged weapons,
With a breath of destruction that can bend ones perception into the void of illusions.
filled with shackles that silence and seals any known tongue to man
with forbidden signs from a rotten template written from the rays of the sun.

Stating that only fears is what your skin will taste,
A pleasant aroma of despair that drills through the layers of your face.
Therefore naivety will be your comforter,
Ignorance will be your shelter,
follishness will be your savior
And obliviousness will be your trusted companion.
.
So doodle more or less for life will still be an ignorant mess.

Locked up

I'm being locked up to rust,
holding my own tomb and sleeping in the dust .
I thought it was a luck of love but it was just an aroma of lust,
So tell me how can I adjust when I am filled with misery and disgust
For the moment I have a broken trust a fragile heart that is continuously being crushed.

So if anyone is there...
Open the door for me and give me a light,
For I have been sitting here without a daylight,
Every moment my own sight is pitch black as the night,
It makes me insane for this room is painful and tight,

My solemn request is to unlock this door,
a glimpse of hope with an assurance that I'll be alright
For where I am been spending my days are infinite terrors and sorrors unite.

Stellar Eyes

The way you look at me with those candid stellar eyes,
I already seen through you a pitch neon shadow in disguise.

I'm horrified and trembled by the grip of that ferocious gaze,
It cause my time sinks with an immense delayed.

You're an unbolted door,
The truths of mirrors,
likely a menace towards the swords of my riddles.

Therefore my lips will go numb for years as my ears taste a depth of your sensational fears,
For I am instinct with a shallow bond of our blood mixture with hazy dreadful tears.

Arun Bhagat

I hung up my boots last year as Associate Professor and Head, Department of English, DAV Centenary College, Faridabad, Haryana, India, after having taught English to college students for forty years. Have been an avid reader since my younger days and have also done a lot of writing work as a part of my professional duties. I started writing poetry some eight years ago but the process has accelerated over the last couple of years. I write poems both in English and Hindi and have my poetry blog on WordPress where I publish my poems regularly. With the Almighty's grace, writing poetry on diverse issues which act as a trigger and rhyming come quite naturally to me now and I thoroughly enjoy the very process and act of writing and thereby having stimulating conversations with my readers.

What is Poetry?

Poetry is a sacred prayer,
It is not a string of words mere!
It is the harbinger of a lost rapture,
The essence of life does for us it capture!
It is a form of meditation,
It draws us out of every agitation!
It takes us out of the gloomy prison of our days,
It shows us of liberating freedom the ways!
Our consciousness does it certainly raise,
It shows us a way out of life's troubling maze!
The mundane it helps us transcend,
Into the sordid chaos of life it does not let us descend!
Our festering wounds it heals,
To the sordidness of life a decisive blow it deals!
It transforms a curse into a blessing,
Such is its power and such its exquisite dressing!
It pulls us out of the vortex of hate,
With the higher sensibilities of life it helps us keep a date!
Let a thousand poems bloom
To pull us back from the edge of doom!

Bring Your Love into Action

Bring your love into action,
That is how it will gain traction!
Let your love transcend all factions,
Let it flow freely through all sections!
Lived love is the best,
That will put all speculation about its existence to rest!
If you trust someone, offer some proof
Lest your trust be considered a mere spoof!
Let that trust sparkle in your eyes,
Doing that will surely be something wise!
What is regret without corresponding change?
Just a hollow vessel strange!
Let love, trust and regret manifest themselves in your behaviour,
And,believe me, they will prove to be your saviour!

Let No Thoughts Cloud over Your Heart

Your heart is the moon,
Hope you realise it soon!
Let no thoughts cloud over it,
They with your heart ill-fit!
Let the moon shine forth in all its glory,
Let it tell its own wonderful story!
Let it spread of love the warm glow,
Let it through every vein and pore of your being flow!
Let no dark thoughts overwhelm your heart,
Let not them pierce it like a dart,
Lest it should lose its bearing
By cringing from every morbid thought and it fearing!
Let the stream of thoughts flitting across your heart go their way
Lest they it overpower and sway.
Do not engage with them and they will fade away
Barring here and there a thought stray,
And then the moon of your heart will be out with all its magic
As it will have averted a fate most tragic!

Demolish The Walls That Exist In Your Mind

Demolish the walls that exist in your mind,

And to yourself be kind!

Once these walls are down, you will be free and happy,

There will then be no need for you to be of others suspicious and snappy!

These illusory walls impede of your life the flow,

They don't let you live uninhibited and glow!

They don't let you the whole existence embrace,

They do not let you bask in God's infinite grace!

They don't let you be kind and good to all,

They make you into the morass of needless ill-will and animus fall!

Walls block the sunlight of good sense,

They make you see others through a crooked and distorted lens!

So let us all walls bring down and shun

So that,rising above our delusional separateness, we can be happy together and one!

Athul P

Athul P, hailing from Angadipuram, Malappuram district of Kerala, was born on 1993 as son of Geetha and Pavithran. He completed his M. Phil degree in Social Work from Delhi University. His first collection of poems 'Epiphanies of an Indian love' is available in amazon KDP. His short story in Malayalam was published in 'Samakalika Malayalam' weekly. He is a contributor in some English and Malayalam web portals as well.

Dairy of a Lover

Every night, when I finally sleep,
I promise to myself, no more pain.
The very next day, frozen waves of
pain, wake me up on the rise.
When I open my windows, your
memory triggers even in the most unlikely visuals.
A cup of water traces the map
of grief inside.
My body, your fellow traveler to
constellation, finds itself stiff to
hold a brush.
A shower, very much similar to the one
before funeral.
Breakfast, like my days, tasteless.
The monuments of our memories await
me on the way to my work.
My heartbeats, no more bother being late.
I find a narrow passage between
the conscious and unconscious in the files
I meditate,
only to get illuminated to your absence later.
My body shies away from the rays of a setting sun
to a coffee shop.
There, the tempo of my sips
portray the velocity of my seconds.
Walking back,
my hands search for yours
and waves through a parallel road of
meaninglessness in air.
Dinner,

the candles we shared
burning alone in me.
Me and my bed seems like two lonely companions.
Incomplete in your absence.
And every night when I finally sleep,
I promise to myself, no more pain.

Avuyile Tshiseka

My name is Avuyile Tshiseka and I am 14 years old. I live in an African community where poetry is the only way of expressing myself. I have one sibling and am an only girl in my family. I go to Gonubie High School and my favorite subject is English. I enjoy reading a lot and also love singing. I also enjoy debating as I want to be a lawyer one day. My favorite color is black because it has a way of expressing how I usually feel. I'm a food addict and enjoy home cooked meals. Poetry is my way of expressing myself in ways I never can in words.

Did you have to be?

Did you have to be so cruel
Did you have to be so real
Did you have to be so painful
And did you have to be so hateful

I still needed them in my life
I still wanted them to alive
You took them from me
And had no eyes to see

The pain u caused
Could never go untold
I tried to move on
But felt so lone

You gave so much hate
More than one could take
You lacked so much compassion
That could use a companion

Oh death
You are a heavy case
That I wanna forget
But I know will never be
gone.

Momma I'm sorry

I know I let you down
I put down your crown
I should've been there
I should've cared

I remember your words of pain
As fast as they came
You said them in hope
That I'd one day cope

But I didn't care
I never cared
I wanted to live my life
No matter how sharp the knife

You wanted what you thought was best
And I gave you my worst
I left you in tears
Not caring how it hurt

And today I wanna say sorry
I never meant to let you down
I wanted my own crown
But momma I'm sorry

Too good to be true

You came when I least expected you
When I thought love wasn't true
I saw you as an imposter
Trying to make me into a poster

I knew I loved you
But my feelings of hurt wouldn't let me
I doubted you
Your love I didn't see

But you proved me wrong
You showed me love after so long
I let you in like no one else
And you showed me your true self

We've been through so much together
My heart as light as feather
Your love healed my pain
And I'm sure we both gained

I know I shouldn't
I should see u as my prince in a suit
But I can't help but wonder
If this love is too good to be true

Beauty in pain

Dear pain
I know I should call you lame
But I somehow can't live
Without you in my life

You bring power to my smile
And make it seem a mile
You bring tears to my eyes
That make it easier to hide my lies

Without you I wouldn't be happy
You've taken over me
And driven me crazy
U make me see who I wanna be

Without you I'd have no purpose
I'd see no point in promises
No joy in my smiles
And no affection in my laughs

I know you think you're hurting me
And sometimes you do
But Pain
I see beauty in you

Ayesha Abdul Kader

Ayesha Abdul Kader is from India. She is Housewife. Mother of 2 kids. Poem writing is her passionate hobby. She has a dream of publishing her own poetic book in future.

Angels on Earth

It was time for her next shift,
Preparing herself for the battle.
Taking care of her attire,
Wearing those n95 masks.
Walking towards the ward,
With huge files in her hand.
Each patient had a mild view,
Half breathe away from soul.
Considering each one with care,
Was the only option she had.
Sweating inside her battle-kit,
Tried to pump oxygen for needy.
Suppressing her cough ,
Ran towards the emergency call.
Closing many eyes forever,
With her tearful heart felt hands.
End of the shift was tiring,
Removing each stuff with care.
Disposing those medical waste,
Keeping herself safe.
So that she can prepare again,
For the next shift ahead.
Being Angels on Earth,
Fighting against the Virus.

Read with Love

Walking through veranda,
Towards Library.
Intention was sure,
To accomplish next Novel.
Reading was a passion,
Grabbing each book with thrill.
Grasping each line on page,
With mere Smile on face.
Eager was the mind,
To finish the book soon.
It was an achievement,
Finishing each book with a lesson.
That was school time,
Spending most time in Libraries.
But now time has changed,
No more reading rooms.
Books are on cell phone.
And Novels on Screen.
Wish for Reading is rare,
Just the climax is known.
Time is rushing for each one,
With scheduled class.
Online life is crucial to manage ,
With a glimpse of Reading.

C-section

An unusual feeling all around,
As if I am paralyzed.
Resonant sound outside,
Makes me confused.
Yes; it's decided,
And I am being prepared.
White arms came near me,
To stop my uncontrolled moves.
My eyes tried to rest,
Still forcefully I stood awake.
Something happening,
Across my tummy.
Within no seconds,
I heard the voice of my world.
My eyes wandered all around,
To have a glimpse sight.
There came my tiny hero,
Wrapped in sister's arms.
I just had a view,
Then again I was left empty.
But having a hope in mind,
To meet my shining star soon.

Life line

It's too late,

For an extra thought over mind.

Disappointed face pointed,

Shedding Tears on eyes.

Ego and Jealousy broke out,

In front of those silence.

No more funny laugh,

And no more teasing words.

Love and Care patiently waited,

For the changes ahead.

Ego realized the fact,

And Jealousy saw the truth.

No man is Forever in the world,

So it's better to be like Love.

Time can never be re-winded,

So let's hold hand with Care.

Maybe many were left alone,

Because of harsh Egotism.

And many lead their life unhappily,

Through interference of Jealousy.

It’s all about mere sacrifice,

Until now and then.

It’s ok to be Genuine and Guilty too,

Before it’s too late....

Camina Kruger

Hey guys, I am Camina Kruger poet signature: Ck-writings... I really hope you like my poem. I love to write and especially about things people relate to or can learn from. I am currently doing a teaching degree but I hope this will be a way for me to create a name for myself. Enjoy!

The End is to come

I prayed over the Bible today,
Although I had no words.
I prayed over the Bible today,
and God told me to expect the worst.
I begged over the Bible today,
And I asked God to keep us safe.
I cried over the Bible today
And all I wanted was peace .
I asked my God for answers
I asked him for forgiveness although I had so many chances.
I spoke to God today and he made sure I felt his presence
He had made it clear to me that if I open my eyes I will have a chance to see the heavens
I asked God to hold my hand as we are facing dark times
We are surrounded by looters and other deadly crimes
We are separated by our color, our religion and our wealth
Things that do not matter when we will have to answer for ourselves.
I have learnt that on the last day God will not ask me why I was not rich.
But what God will ask is why I was not secure with in Him.
Why did I not believe, so I could recieve his grace.
Why did I not search his word and beg to see his face

The last days are near but I refuse to live in fear. For God so loved the world that he gave his one and only Son, that whoever believes in him shall not perish but prosper and have eternal life. .

Charles R LaFevre

Charles R La`Fevre.
Born 1954 Bucks County Pennsylvania
Been writing since childhood
never published
many writing lost
many never shown

Do not cry

Do not ask why
Nothing is forever
Lets be thankful for our time together
Nothing is forever, that is the reason why
Do not cry, Look at the sun in the sky
Smile as you remember the good times
Never ask why, We all will die
Our time here is is short
Let us be thankful for the time together

Every breath is another moment of survival

I seek you as a lover, not a rival
For together we learned the art of survival.
Survival of love
Over the Rival of Despair
gives us our moment as a Pair

I am

I am the child of hopes and dreams
I am the son, My father's child
Born of hopes and dreams
Grown to be wild, I am the child
I am my father's hopes and dreams
I am Me

Chelsea Doss

Chelsea, or better known as C. R. Doss, is a passionate writer hailing from the Virginia Blue Ridge Mountains. Her poetry is rooted in nature, philosophy and relationships. She lives her life by this simple mission, to live purposefully, love relentlessly, and pursue passionately the things that both rapture and rupture your soul. She is eternally grateful to share with you some of her heart's work.

Rare Breed

We are a rare breed,
You and I,
Seeing the world through the hands of philosophers
and poets,
Allowing those like Emerson and Plath,
to cultivate and mold us,
From the rest, our pottery make look a little
different,
But our material, what we are made of,
is unequivocally significant.

Indentations

I can't wait
for that one day
when I wake up
and find
the pillow next to me
has indentations
from where
you were,
from where,
I wanted you to be.

Noteworthy

I may not be noteworthy,
but I am willing...
to allow a melodic deconstruction,
and you...
for you, to replace,
my chromatic scaled position,
substituting your nuanced composition,
transposed into being only yours,
and passionately titled:
"My Love: a Revived Rendition"

To Move On

It was in our stillness,
that deep penetrating silence,
we found our forgiveness,
an unspoken willingness,
to move on.
Better off alone.

Chibueze Moses Junior

I'm a student of University of Nigeria, Nsukka. I'm presently in the department of Zoology and Environmental Biology. My hobbies are reading, composing poems, researches and listening to music.

Africa

Africa! The home of the beautiful sun
Harrumph! The elephants trumpet with pride
They beat their giant feet majestically on their native soil
The home of beautiful lush vegetation
Though the skies be reddened
You shall sing again
The birds shall make music again
Your children shall be proud of you once again
Africa! The big womb that birthed our fathers
The home of the Nile
Where men march as warriors with the power of universe against the axis of evil
Home of brave hunters with their poisoned darts
They face the Big Cat and make it tremble in fear
Africa! The home of soulful musicians
Upon your sacred soil
Fela Anikulapo trod
As he battled servitude with his life
His life meant little to him
Only your children mattered to him
Upon your sacred soil
Nelson Mandela trod
A beacon of hope to the hopelessly helpless
He fought chains gallantly and won you a medal
Upon your sacred soil
Chinua Achebe trod,
With his brothers Samuel Ajayi Crowder, Kanu Nwankwo, Jay jay Okocha
What about the giantess Dora Akunyili?

Your soil is fertile and blessed
It grows greatness
Africa! Soon you'll be the pride of the World

Sochima (Only God knows)

Who knows
Whether the wounded eagle will fly again?
Whether the chick that had gone astray will find its mother again?
Whether the ugly vulture will be beautiful again?
Whether the songbird will let out it's melody again?
Whether the owl will chime its mournful hoots again?
Who knows
Whether the flower will bud again?
Whether the dried grass will be green again?
Whether the banana tree will stand, tall and proud once again?
Who knows
Whether the river that has nowhere to go will flow again?
Whether the dried stream will receive strength again?
Whether the stream that has lost its source will reunite again?
Who knows
Whether the blind will see the beautiful sun again?
Whether the deaf will hear the drumbeats of life again?
Whether the dumb will sing musical melodies larger than life again?
Whether the crippled will touch the sky again?
Who knows
Whether the sun will shine again?
Whether the rainbow will color the earth again?

Whether the slender rain will visit the earth again?
Whether the moon will bathe the earth with its beauty again?
Who knows
Whether the poor will taste good again?
Whether he that sleeps under the bridge will know comfort again?
Whether the orphans will know love again?
Whether the insane will enjoy family again?
Who knows whether the young shall grow again?

David Yusuf

Reading, writing and making speeches.

Deep Down

This pain has bash a hole in me
My day is even darker than my cloudy night
Nightmare seems better than the rising sun if all day remain like this
Prefer a world of fantasy than this ugly reality
Nothing just seems to fall to my plans, not even a bird in hand to compare to thousands in bush
Haven't kill any while ask to kill two with a stone
What a depth of unfairness
Wish I had a choice before birth
Would have prefer the loneliness in the womb
This disappointment here and there
Does nothing more than to kill my hope
Thought I was strong little did I know how weak I am
Have always encourage many yet from within am been discourage
Have comfort many but not even a bird to sing to my distress
The unfairness of life is killing my faithfulness
I work hard, labor more and even put my brain to work
Yet I see nothing, just emptiness
I go out with a mask of smile but the space inside is occupy with emptiness and loneliness, Pain more that no one understand this just me and me alone
Isn't death a rest if compare to this,
Life seems to be a waste of time
What else could I do that family will see that am only giving my best

Dad seems disappointed always not encouraging at all mom thinks I have join them
Make me want to go mad even more
But deep down I am certain am giving it my best but my big question is why can't they see it from my view
Feel like ending it all and erase me from their memory with the tick tock of time
Maybe that best or someone come save
Tell me just one thing
Let me that better days are ahead is just time. .

Dishani Kar

Hello I am Dishani.
I am currently a student and I love to express my thoughts with the help of poetries...

Scars to Wars

The scars in the ruins has something to say,
Close your eyes and feel the fears ,
Of those who died and shed their hopeless tears...
A single scar can tell you the whole story,
Of the betrayal , hatred and someone's shattered glory...
This world with no lights and deep hatred is at fault,
But the scars remind u not to replicate your mistakes and giving them a permanent halt...
The scars and bloodbaths on the walls can take us back to the history,
They can even remind us of the silhouettes of the soldiers and their misery....
The scars are helpful to learn more,
But can't we just avoid these scars from the beginning and live more...
Scars also have disadvantages,
The trust cannot be earned again , just as in the pot with cracks has no advantages...
Because to tell you the scars can also be beautiful,
It can depict the most beautiful things on the earth,
The love and friendship are all it's worth...
Can't we just not turn scars to war and let everyone pay ,
It will turn scars beautiful this way...

Emi Fitri Audina

Emi is a young poet by heart and a preschool teacher by profession. She enjoys writing to express herself, to heal from the pass wound, and to find solution in the quietest way possible.

Jealous

Once you handed me two bottles of yogurt,
I said I deplore a ‘plural’,
like when you put my name next to her.
I don’t know if that’s the same things,
but I have been the second best all my life.
And please not for you too.

Girl's with Daddy's issue

If only you hug me a little tighter,
Before you left to work.
I would never beg temporary people to stay.
Cause that’s how I grew up with,
Love is earned,
in dribs and drabs.

Sad girl 2 am conversation

You never sent me a cute good morning text nor we set nicknames for each other.
I thought there, when things went all wrong.
Until it's 2am, I was wide awake.
And my thought rushed into those days,
You were always one phone call away. You never asked why I was sad.
You knew I was sad half of my life, and without questions you listened to every rant.
I thought the 2am deep conversation with tears in our cheeks, are disposable.
Replaceable to cute good morning text.

Until I realized, They aren't.

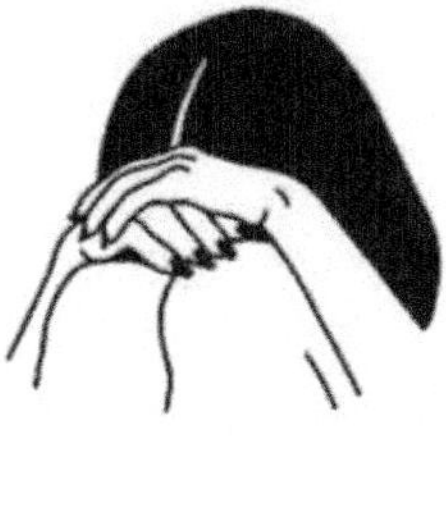

Evidence M Shavi

Evidence M Shavi is a generous, lovely and dramatic guy, who loves writing to an extend of spending his honeymoon on writing.

Humanity and World

Drinking syrup in disguise, iam tired.
I need real life.
Real love, real people and real world.
The art of being human is tough.

Failing and failing is fun and fascinating.
Changing my views drastically and
making myself think from a different
point of view.
Seeing the world and the people around
differently.
Opening up to certain questions.
Putting myself in touch with my
higher nature.

Trying new things, new tricks, that brought
me down from trees and took me to the
moon.
Creating my tools and then my tools
creates me.
Blaming myself of being bewitched by
the unknown person.
Memorising the ideas of the living legends
and those who passed away.
Showing myself that, i make the world.
Studying you all times in all place
is my genre.

Rebuking the idea of ethnocentrism.
Denying being trapped with the little

opportunity to change and grow.
Participant observation is my key in
suspending judgement, and try to
understand the world.
Supporting the antidote of
ethnocentrism can lead us to world
relations widely.

I speak softly and smoothly, as if unware
of that, iam lobbing intellectual fire bombs
into the people and the blowing minds.
Iam spreading out my bunch of ideas to
the world.
Iam being real and open to the world and
expect both results in return.
Every place in this world has its own charm
and can be found in the spirit of the people.

Fighting the confusion despite that, their actions
and greetings looks like an
exuberant and kind greetings.
Sometimes i hear them talking about me
in Tok Pisin in Papua New Guinea.
Speaking in my own language again i
heard them.
This is confusing, i need to know this
world.
If there are different people in different continents
who can run 400 miles without taking a rest,
making friends
with elephants and reaching their goals.
Why cant i?.

Francisco Ramon Bueno

Francisco Ramon Bueno has always found himself drawn to artists. He is a self-taught guitarist who was always into the idea of singing and making his own lyrics, but never pursued it. He hopes to one day create an album with his collection of talented friends. Valentine's Day of 2021 he wrote his first poem for a friend in a card. They really liked it so he decided to keep going and see where his written words will take him.

Instagram:
@cisco_ramon_poetry

Butterflies

Carry me away
To a distant memory
A feeling in my heart, a warmth tingling beneath the soul
I'll catch you if I can, elusive as you flutter
Your beauty leaves me paralyzed and speechless as I stutter
Caterpillar, metamorphosize before my eyes?
Careful on your journey I hear your wings could bring demise
I live for the chaos of hurricanes and butterflies

Galaxies-

The life inside of me is not aware it's not alone
Black hole in my center feeds, but remains unseen
Racing through the universe binarily we may collide
The distance to my relatives grows further in between
I must be original, I'm made of all these pieces
The lights fade in the distance one day I'll be part of history
I'll end in a deep freeze
Join the land of make believe
Am I here again?
Remain the universes mystery

Aphrodite

Wounded at war for the battle of the gods I saw a
dove and for the moment remembered what peace
was
Blood in hands from my sword, she reveals herself
and delivers a white rose
Time freezes, the blood on my hands is absorbed
from the rose and the white rose is now red
How can this be? Have I lost my mind? Have I
really been at war? Am I dead?
I drop my sword, she said “come with me”, time
still frozen, I follow her off the battlefield
All I’ve known in the years of war was hatred for my
enemy
Beautiful goddess, show me how to love.
Swords clashing, enemy war cries, burning cities.
What am I fighting for?
Show me the pleasures in life, I’ll take your hand
and never look back

Show me how to live.

Therapy

Who will be the one who understands me?
In this world we're all alone
Tell me all you think you know
Share with me the ways I can grow

I wonder what I'll tell you next?
The world on my shoulders, I feel it in my chest
I told you too much, should I say less?
With you I feel free, here's the rest...

It never really works that way
The ones I confide in, seldom stay
I understand that life goes on
Thank you for making me feel like I belong

Send me on my way
Tomorrow is another day.

Autumn leaves-

You've got me mesmerized

The way you fall's like a gentle breeze

First I was hypnotized

The heat from summer has me on my knees

I love you, don't want you to leave

You are the air that I breathe

The current is cooler that comes from the ocean

The holidays come getting closer to freeze

Each day I get closer to you, but same time, I leave you behind

You are my partner in mischief, the pinnacle of my remembered times

Pumpkin I carved you, don't fade by the day

In photographs you'll live, please stay

I notice as this goes on, I'm losing the Sun

Are you on the run?

Winter is coming

Gabrielle Pinto

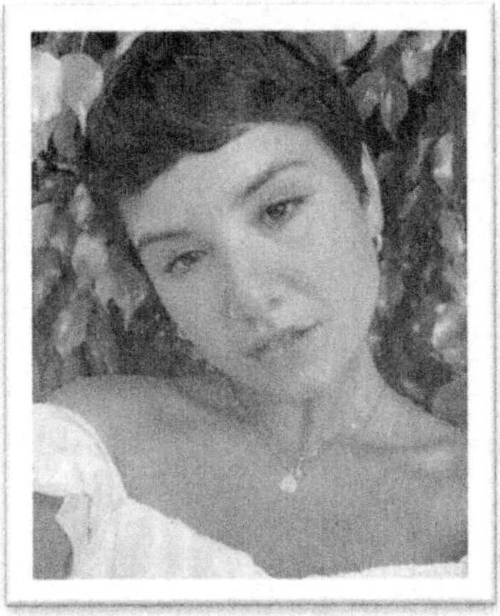

Gabrielle has been a writer for seven years now and is in the process of releasing her first collection. Her work is inspired by past life experiences, and subconscious thoughts. Her work explores themes of duality, perception, and interpretations. Writing has been her coping mechanism despite life altering changes one constant remains and it's her desire to connect her emotions with the observations of the outside world.

You're Logical and I Am Pure Emotion

You're logical and I'm pure emotion.
Everything has to make sense to you,
while I'm content with the unknown.
Your mind works in numerical equations on a chalk board.
I see the authors purpose.
I could show you a painting,
and you could tell me the exact shade of blue the painter used,
and the angle he held his paint brush.
But you can't tell me what inspired him.
Your mind can't contemplate how perpetual the thought of life and death is.
You're too focused on the dynamics of our universe,
but cant fathom the possibility of God.
You see the "how" in everything but not the "why."

Gilbert Matolokoshi

Gilbert was born in Zambia in the flourishing mining town of Solwezi; North Western Zambia. He attended Solwezi Boys High school and completed grade twelve in 1988.After college where. He did a two year course in General Agriculture. After working on commercial farms for many years Gilbert left his country.
Married to Sylvia, they have two grown-up sons. Currently lives in the idyllic city of Cape Town. Hobbies include writing, reading, music, sightseeing and visiting exotic resorts.

Attribute of all Humans

When I set sight on you
My heart throbbed within me
Was stunned and thrilled
You drilled a hole in to my soul
You filled my old bones' cold marrow with fire
You seem as a dream to me
Your name i barely mention
In a mute sort of whisper
Like a sublime dream
I dare not scream
Least the dream flees away
You occur in a vision screen
Streamed in pure rays
Hues transcending the blues
Colors of artistic canvas display
Articulate masterpiece pics
Impeccable with no seams
An aura of sunbeam

A sheer male imagination

An allure, rare sight

Intricate, resolute, intriguing

Aquiline pencil outline

You're blend of races

Trend of racial colors

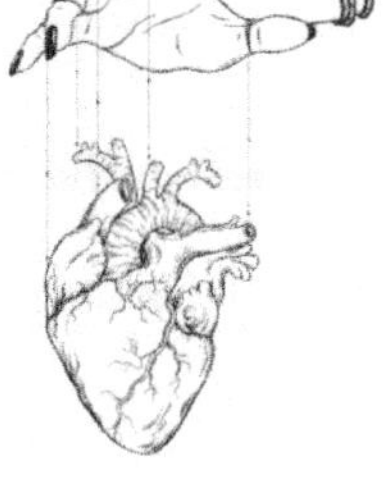

Pretensions to Genius

Generation X bogus mania

Nations of intricate architects

Drilled in all sorts of diametrically

Aligned manoeuvres in disingenuous trickery

Well paired,snugly as romantic lovers

Whereas, singly spouses of different houses

Some pretend as astute industry captains

In reality simply carers of countryside goats

Don't wipe my backside, i conjure your own

Masterplan in this creative game

Am not to blame

Just a mere narrator

Generation X bogus mania

Nations of ingenious morons

Masters in their peculiar games

Of disguise and pure surprise

Each one of these intrepid wizardry

A genius at guise play

Theatrical masked dramatic troupes

Dressed charitably as nobly lords

Mere hoardes of subordinates

Attaired fashionably

As well-to -do , meanwhile

Ordinary and equally poor

Generation rated genius mania

Nations of intriguing thrillers

Poised as muiltimillionairs

Still unable to afford

One bloody million dollars

Some still devising ways

To win a billion dollar jackpot

Whimsical ones, American dream dreamers

Grown-up young at heart

Waiting to inherit wealth

By any means that be;

Crook or hook period

Gomathi Seetharaman

Age : 40
Hobby: Hiking
Passion : Exploring mother nature

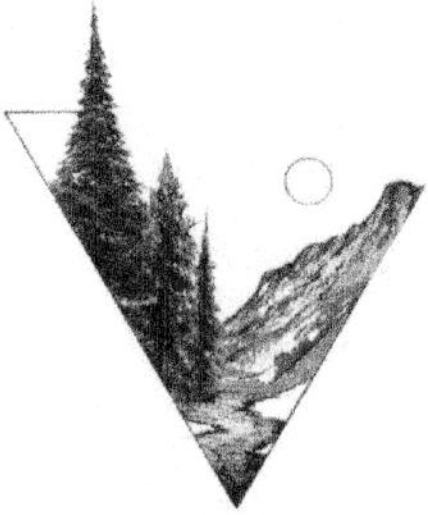

Perhaps

Finding my way,
If I could go back in time today....
way before yesterday,
To search and find myself in right way before my first kiss and touch,
I wish to see your eyes before I close my eyes,
Yet, I find my world has crushed into the hidden darkness...
The voice inside me left no clue...
Just how much I think that I try to hide
As what as I told you before...
Perhaps !! You might stay to be the same way.

Disappointed

I miss you,
In every beat of my heart,
In every blink of my eyes,
I don't give you the pain,
I will do anything for you,
Please don't break my heart,
I do have feelings like you,
Where it went wrong,
Until you need to hold my throat and kill me,
Why I need to die without reason,
I still do have feelings like humans,
But, why it always have to be us to carry the suffering?
I can carry a loyalty where no other humans can carry.

Stir

Sometimes you meet someone and it is so clear that... the two of us ...on some level that we belong together.
Being honest to be with you it's the first sparkle in my heart....
It does speak a lot in my empty mind....
As a dream come alive on me...
Plan and ideas which cannot be understood whether to be as a lovers or friends or entirely different.
I just work up.... down to earth every day to be with you....
Because I love you.

Gredually Maphanga

I am Gradually Maphanga, 20 years old my love for poetry started when I was 17. I am from South Africa in Mpumalanga province

She....

She is what you'd call a goddess
Elegant as a rose
Voice so sweet it warms my heart
Strong like a bull yet delicate as a fairy
Eyes so bright like a star in the sky
She wore the armer of love itself
And she welds the sord of justice
She marked my heart with the kiss of faith
She took my heart and sealed it away
She is the reason am on side sighted
For my eyes see no one but her
She evaded my thoughts
I can't think of anyone but her
She is the one I long for

Why?...

Why would you show me light? Just to leave me in the dark

Why would you give me happiness? Just to replace it with sadness

Why you show me love

Only to take it away from me

You stood by me on summer's day

But on winters day you fled away

Even your shadow couldn't find you If you knew you were going to leave

Why not teach me to live without you

Why not teach me to love another

If you were just passing by

Why didn't you let me know from the start? Why did I let in my heart to begin with? From now on nothing comes in my heart

And nothing comes out, no more love! We were in love together, but why

Do I bare this pain alone, no more love! If you come with your love to me

Please keep it, no more love for me

Please used that love and love yourself I am done with love

Gregory Hills

Gregory Hills age 66 and lives alone in the mid-western USA. An addictions therapist for 28 years and a former professional drummer and singer. He enjoys composing music, lyrics and poetry; bicycling, camping and photography; and, visiting family and friends. He has been writing poetry on a consistent basis for about
three years.

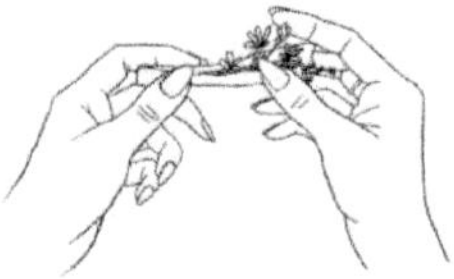

Her name was Laniakea (Immeasurable Heaven)

Many lifetimes ago, when
I was a light keeper on an Atlantean island,

I was friends with a woman named
Laniakea, who was beloved amongst our people.

Some mornings, melodies would form
from her countenance into floating poems.
Sometimes
i would catch them
before they disappeared, preserving them

for the fishermen to take
on their lonely journeys.

In this present life, she and I have never met;
but we speak through a
slower-moving ether, where her

blue eyed sky
is beheld in the golden palm of
mornings, and her raven hair

whispers past my
still-photo memory

In The Year 2134

The cloud people waited,
for me to evaporate into prayer

for rain

I fell,
to speak into the ears
of the man I want you to see

with a new name, more gentle than
the last; surrounded by a sea

of deepest intention, and ancient
will.

I don't believe it's a miracle
that you found me

Messages from the First Parents

When the messages from first parents stopped
coming in black and white,

I stopped taking sides
against shadows; remembered

my future and her name

she hummed a blue crystal
firefly that led me

into a pool by a mill; where I bathed to take
all my memories away,
save one

how to find and make love to the earth,
again
so she could give birth to heaven

For Dayna

I won't love you as
a lover, a betrothed, or even a
passing crush.

And even if I
were to build us a window
from the waves of sand in heaven;
it won't won't reveal us anywhere,
but in a few moments, where

our little friendship
has found a home,
in some glowing infinity

Hafiszh Ayyashy

Hafiszh Ayyashy is an Indonesian poet who works in Data Analytics. He has a passion for analyzing and writing literature. He is on a journey to establish friendship with uncertainties and to find meaning in the overlooked aspects of life.

Favourite Quote: "Speak the truth, even when your voice shakes" - Maggie Kuhn

Instagram - fishy_poetry

No Man's Laws

A needless trial
with a jury of unjustifiable bias, selected through an invalid voir dire

Devoid of rational precedence, there is no statute of limitations to how long emotions may cease to exist

No one should be prosecuted
for withholding arbitrary feelings, which often come unpremeditated

Governed by their own jurisdiction,
one's despair and desire obey no man's laws

A co-signed affidavit between two parties, is never immune to disputes

In this case,
the judge who hammered the final verdict
should have been none other than the defendant himself

Garden of Eden

We planted this

A seed that seeks
polluted water

Enveloped by unwelcoming soil,
its roots took detours
to reach much needed nutrients

Bludgeoned by unforgiving sunlight,
it perseveres to grow

And once in a blue moon,
flowers bloom

And the cycle continues

White Noise

Ears; deafened by echoes
of freedom fighters

The roars of desperate, unfortunate souls
are no longer heard

Albeit, the service has stopped operating for a good
while

An eerie epiphany:
What if the leaf-shaped organ
was intended to only be receptive to words of the
higher echelons?

In the sea of silence,
words tend to drown
never finding their way back to the surface

Rhythmically Challenged

A creaky ballroom,
inside an abandoned theatre
A hall of gloom,
with no dancer

Courageous steps forward,
with no promised reward
Cowardly steps backward,
with nothing but hazard

This music;

A phony euphony;
A dissonance
masquerading as a harmonious brilliance

Quarrels of melodies
in my head;
uncooperative rhapsodies
loud as lead

This sound I wish to mute,
numbs my ears in absolute

Hannah Kircher

Hannah is a 21 year old born and raised in North Carolina. There is nothing she loves more in life than to express herself creatively. From painting, writing, singing, modeling, etc. She is always turning the imagination into her reality.

Soulmate

Every stage of the sun and moon
I'm happiest to know that I am next to you
I thank the stars for living in your eyes
And filling mine with a twinkle of life
There's no other person I'd want to spend every life time together with.

Forever and Always

Our flesh and bones
Will grow flowers over a field
And our love will run through the universe
And cosmic skies
For we will die
But our love will last forever
And our souls will intertwine
Always,
We will find each other again.

Jasper A. Requiso

Jasper A. Requiso is an antiquated teen
he likes old songs, and stuff.
He loves to play the words in Rhyme.

The Candle was "I"

There was a candle that was "I"
Lighted by a match to give some fire
Warm heat to hug all I have
Burn my sadness and gives some love

The candle were being lighted
A reddy orange bright
That fills every heart
And ready to wear & give a smile

But the candle cried
He takes all the pain & hide
Wanting to fade as the darkness bide
To lose the light as the light died

Somehow the candle loss its light
Eaten by sorrows and griefs
To make the candle fumble
For the light is only a brief light

Now the candle has no light
It is covered by a dimmed light
Don't know where to go either left or right
He lose the battle for he don't fight

And then the candle saw its like
A new kind that tooks its spike
He then look at its light
And cried for it's beautiful to give some light.

Jeff Flesch

Jeff grew up in Los Angeles, California, and now lives in Corvallis, Oregon where he works in education. Jeff's writing interests and passions include personal and professional development, developing new ways to increase access to higher education, and creating inspiration, transformation, and more equity throughout society. Jeff has two very creative and inspirational sons, which are his pride and joy. You can reach Jeff at jeffflesch.com.

Grass Tethers

Grass Tethers tears
collected from
the grass tethers,
weathered,
many a storm
have they,
resurrected now,
and forever

more

they grow
straight,
and tall,
and when
pushed aside, they
always abide
in the knowing
inside.

Our Hearts Guide

Our Hearts Guide
as the ground
cracks
beneath me, I'm
reminded,
of the fissures
running along
the entirety of
my being.

cracks that,
at times,
become craters,
wide, with unknown
depths
just like the earthly
realm we see, full
of paths on land,
and under the sea.

cracks
and craters
stepped,
and leapt over,
I'm now moving
beyond times measure.

unknown distance
from the center,

and yes,
hard to measure.

scraping
and clawing
our way into that
center, is
of utmost pleasure,

and pain, both.

yet,
what other way
would we have it?

inside the depths
of those fissures
lies the heart
of another life
lived, discarded,
and now, intentionally
picked back up for progression.

moving again,
in synchronicity,
as we glide,
we will abide,
and once again follow
our hearts guide

Jitesh Sinha

Jitesh Sinha is an entrepreneur. He has a bit of sarcasm in his tone; he is funny ready for adventure, hardworking guy. He loves what he does, he is also mentoring 3 startups and always up for gaining knowledge. He has just gotten into writing apart from this he loves dancing, travelling and photography!!! Once you get to know him you will really like him.....

Secret

Today I'm gonna tell you a secret that no one else in the world knows,
I m a kid from heart who whips and cry when talks to you that's my secret!
I m a demanding baby when it comes to you, that's my secret!
I'm an arrogant man when I'm upset, that's my secret!
I fantasize about you when I'm high, that's my secret!
I feel bad when you talk about your guy friends to me, that's my secret!
I feel bad when you are sad, but I want you to stay as strong as you are because that keeps me pushing for more hard work, that's my secret!
I always imagine being with you when I take my last breath, that's my secret!
I want to give you all the happiness of the world so sometimes I avoid you and keep working, that's my secret!

Loving you is all I want to do all day long, but I want a better future for us so I ignore you sometimes, that's my secret!
I really love when you get mad at me and I love it because I know that's how u show your love for me, I know that and still ignore it cause I love it, that's my secret!
I love to see your smile that's how I feel cherish and it calms me down so I take screenshots when we

video chat, that's my secret!
And last if all I love you till the moon and back, but many a times I forget to express, I know it I'm heartily sorry for that, cause I know I should do it and I still don't, that's my secret!
One more secret of my life is
I SEE MY MOTHER LOVE IN YOUR LOVE! That's why I'm so afraid to lose you, "THATS MY SECRET"

Kunal Saha

Kunal Saha 17 years old a college student, who lives in Dibrugarh, Assam. He is not so introverted and not so extroverted but he likes to surrounded by his close ones. He likes dancing, writing and reading as well and watching reality shows is the best part of his day. You can say he is a nerd without glasses, though learning new things also includes his passion. Besides his parents, Kunal can't imagine his life without his sister. He is very focused on his carrier and also he thinks he is matured enough compared to other of his age. Still, Kunal has a lot more unfolded story in his life.

Addiction

The journey begins from the first snuff,
One is too many and thousands isn't enough.
Darkness dragged me into that mess
Bleeding nose is also less;
Virtual reality is my primary address.
Joy started from a needle or a bottle of pills,
That's the gutter full of thrills.
After flying so high in the sky,
I think the reality is all a lie.
Feeding my anger is the priority of first,
The destination where everything is cursed
Devil is always craving for more,
Have the fear of inner evil roar.
The formula is twice a dose in a day,
I take thrice instead what they say.
We are strong and we will fight,
Pull out the darkness and take a place in the light.
They will say everything is fine,
When 666 is going to be 999.

Eternal Love

Yelling at the sky,
Screaming at the world.
Past, pushing me into the dark
Landscape was grey and stark
The day with pink sunset arrive,
Her glance forge me alive.
Eyes transparent as cloudless
sky,
That's the girl, makes me high.
Smiling free as a rose in
summer air,
Trying to enfold- you in despair.
Your kiss is a Disney splash,
While the moon holding the
flash.
Stars sticks me to the reality,
If loving you is a fault, yes I'm
guilty.
The night twice beeped to
cross,
Time was riding on a horse.
She eloped with nature,
But for me she is not any
stranger.

Leona Grové

She is someone who has faced many challenges from an early age, but turns it into creativity through her art and poetry. She loves technology and has a big heart for animals. She believes that a person is not limited by their talent, because talent grows the more your passion for something does.She believes in live and let live,be the best human you can be and be true to who you are. You can check out her page on facebook called Leona/Bella/Elena poems,art and photography.

Secrets 2

In broad daylight, I am distracted from all the pain inside.
As the sun sets and I sit up alone at night, the truth manifests.
I feel my heart racing and my mind running extremely wild.
I become anxious like a mother not finding her child.
Breathing deep, eyes closed, I fade into another dimension.
My soul escapes into a dream where no one can invade.
Far away from the constant chaos I endure every day.
Now I can listen with caution what my soul has to say.
My spirit is now free, and the truth of myself I can finally see.
Here I am, a swan glittering under the face of the moon.
I stare to the heavens and realize that I have lost my way.
Yes, I have lost my way, like a falling star, I don't feel okay.
I look down and see blood for there is a feather missing.
I see my tear rolling down my chest, it shines like a diamond.
Like my wound, there is someone that has left a gap in my heart.

Once so close, now feeling like we are a million oceans apart.
The words I feel, appear bright into the darkness of night.
These emotions are the secrets that are only safe within myself.
I love you and I miss you more than any human could bare.
It hurts so bad knowing that next time I fall apart, you won't be there.

Winter

Its winter here and beauty is dying.
The night lasts longer and the day starts late.
Leaves crumble as they are falling.
Can anyone hear my broken voice calling?
It's cold, no flaming love, breaking the ice;
Only illness and sadness roaming in the skies...
My emotions are covered like snow-covered trees.
I only break apart when no one in this world sees.
No more tears for they're as dry as dust.
Only a face smile ripping through my lips.
Can anyone read a story behind eyes so dead?
Wouldn't life be better if everyone in this world
cared?

A Storm and I become one.

As I walk the endless road alone;
No one but me, all on my own...
A storm and I become one.
A broken heart seeks shelter, where there's none.
Flaming heart absorbs tears that do not flow.
An empty soul does not know where to go.
Dark clouds compress until it can't anymore.
Until the drops of bitterness force down to pour.
Chaos arises with colliding sky.
For deep inside I'm left to die.
Lightning, called a beautiful disaster.
A sign of life; my heart beats faster.
Destructive the explosion of pain will be.
A heart too heavy, will force all truth to break free.
The raindrops crash down hard against my face...
Until I'm dry and the truth will find it's hidden
place.

Violent silence

You can be between millions of people;
But yet, you could still feel alone and empty.
You could speak out all your thoughts.
When you're alone, the true you breaks free.
They say that quietness is a way of peace.
In actual fact, silence is a violent pain.
Music is the resurrection of a broken soul.
Don't let the voice within drive you insane.
Don't tell the world that you are hurt.
Don't tell them your world's tumbling down.
Sing a song that you can relate to.
Don't speak of the reason why you frown.
It's not easy living in an empty world.
My hope for you is to find your reflection.
Someone, who could truly understand,.
Someone... who could be your soul's protection.

Lhabab Dorji

Lhabab Dorji is from Bhutan, born on 22 Nov 1980. He is a poet as well as English teacher in Bhutan. He has MA in English Literature. He is member of many poetry society winning awards and certificate such as Certificate of Honor, Achievement, Winner, Excellence, Recognition, Honorable Mention, Medallion De Appreciation, Medallion de Respect. He is a recipient of Independence Day Literary Honor on 15th August 2021 from Motivational Strips. On 31st August 2021, he received Honorary Award for Excellence in Literature and Arts from How to Write for Success Literary Network. On 1st October 2021, he received Independence Honor from GWW Community, Nigeria.

Woman and Her Beauty

The beauty of woman is innumerably untold
If ever to bring forth some in the light of course
The wisest of the soul is the womanly born
To guide the male generation to uplift his soul
And teach them to be the shining star of the world

Though she is femininely controlled by males as known
But her power to control her family is graciously grown
Not letting to witness the downfall of her progeny and man

Although her physical strength is like ebb and flow of tides
But she does more than what man can using her might
And always brighten the heart of all, no matter rich or poor

Her heart is tenderly woven with the silken knot of love
For she sacrifices her morsel for her children and love
And tolerates hunger more than the bullet that hits her
Her love for her man is the blooming flower without season
Always growing stronger and brighter ever with prayer.

To My Mother

A Mother is no ordinary soul
She is emanation of goddess Rhea in fold
A mother is the luminous source of light
Illuminating the pride of child with all her might
She redeems her progeny drowning in insecurity
And in all-weather she struggles as her sole duty
Downfall of child is what she cannot resist
Hard work and perseverance is what she persists
Every word she utters, showers like heavenly sound
Sweetest as Nightingale that is rarely found
A mother's heart is as delicate as feather
Becomes stronger if weather does not favor
Imprinting, mother in heart should be child's vision
If this is forgotten you will be never forgiven.

She Remained in My Heart

The recollection of those jocund days unforgettable
Illuminated our gracious play once not very long
Every subject look upon us for we epitomized our
love
There was no fight and fraught written on our side
Infinitive was our attention loomed for attraction

Even the god of love Cupid peeped with affection
For he found that our love is soothingly sedative
Cried we sometimes for we know our stay is short
And prayed to God to make our love subject to
sought

Our tears are outburst of faith for unconditional
love
And turns into ambrosial dew tasted to test our love
But unpredictable day cunningly succumbed our
play
She closed her eyes to showcase our day in heavenly
stay

My burning heart then sensationally went
paralyzed
She remained in my heart as image of inaccessible
stat afar
And her love imprinted in hearses of my heart
forever
Though you cannot be psychically hugged and loved
My heart always gleams with word, I Love You Still.

The Eagles

Her beauty so enchanting and imprinted
And colonized my heart as angel she depicted
Thinking of castaway love afar drags me crazy
And rhythmically it lures my heart to be dizzy
When I dream of her alluring charismatic beauty
My soul triumphed her presence in bounty
Thus my consciousness soared like the eagles
And gleefully I stumped and danced like the angels.

Linda Jessica Wang

Linda Wang is a university studentstudying Marketing and English. She has a passion for creative writing, nature walks and Christianity. She believes in seeing the beauty in life! Lidia began her spiritual awakening journey at 17 years old. After years of severe social anxiety, spirituality helped her find her authentic voice. She loves to absorb universal energy – like a warm marshmallow – and channel them into gooey, fun, & creative mediums! Check out her blog for creative spiritual spiritual epiphanies: http://www.spiritualfantasia.com! You can also find her on Instagram @spiritualfantasia!

Butterfly Happiness

A positive vibration ripples in life's fabric
Happiness flaps its wings like a butterfly
Soaring across the present moment

Fluttering delicately with joyous wonder
A transformative sight dances colorfully
Brightening each life it encounters

When happiness lands on you
Discover the freedom of its wings
Feel the bliss in each moment

Lynard Sketch

Lynard Sketch is from Kenya. Widely talented, a poem writer, a deejay, a professional journalist. His favorite quote "You can hurt my body but never touch my soul".
His style is unique; he uses nature to talk of the human endeavors.

Petals in the wind

From calm and tenderness
Wind from the west blows
No time nor warning to harness
With no time to prepare for the blows

Plucked from the warmth of its huddle
With no warning thrown away from the bundle
Flying away with no specific direction
No time to gather a linear projection

In the cold and constant rejection
Finding freedom from the ejection
Learning to sway in the wind with no intention
High from the ground a feeling of no obligation

Freedom, loud and clear
Sway with no fear
Focus above and away from anything near
Loosing memories of the warmth so dear

Time passing, energy running low
So fast, so high now in awe
Finally time to take a bow
Back to the ground that was short. wow.

Traces

As I sit down and untie the lace
I get pulled to the details of the race
The race that you set the pace
Trying to be worth your case
But no, to you am worth replace

The cold nights we spent at the stair case
The promises we wrote never to part
The cold brought us together, each other's back we pat
Encouraged to change our lives, we chose a hut

The hut brought us warmth and now we could afford a hat
Our heads we covered, to shield us from the sun
Remember what we said we will name our son?
Our bodies now warm we could afford a smile

Remember the trip we took to the Nile
How wonderful and peaceful was the stream
Here we are now and what I can hear are screams
Whatever went wrong in our dreams

I wake light cast on me from a beam
My energy drained from your scream
It all changed since we tied the lace
Now home is no longer a peaceful place

Is the cold what we deserved?
Because now the warmth feels like a curse

Are our dreams the furnace?
The furnace that feeds your anger

I choose to stand and wait
But am growing faint
Will distance be the new paint
The paint that will color your lost faith?

A Rose in the Wild

Tender,calm,fresh
Soothing,quiet and timid.
In quiet it blossoms,
Morning dew untouched it glitters.
A rose in the wild.

Thorns part of a stem,
Harmless they thrive in the wild,
For the bees a feast of the scent so mild
Tall it stands, loud it is and in nature so bold
A rose in the wild

The color so significant,
Petals gathered together
Warmth of whispers in the gathering
Trust shared, hugs shared as it transcends it's short time
A rose in the wild.

Unattended, unpruned
The journey to beauty was not pretty,
Weed a major interruption,
Stem so green and straight to show passion
A rose in the wild.

As nature giveth so it taketh
One thing clear, it has been heard
Shared smiles and purpose it had
A mark of happiness bundled in its bud
A story of a rose in the wild.

Madhurra Deshmukh

The author of the poem The Deserted Love is Madhurra Deshmukh.She lives in Hyderabad, India.She has written many poems and some have been published too.She is originally from Nagpur,India.Her hobbies are reading, photography, painting,long walking and music .She has done some social work related to health.From childhood she was interested in writing and wrote many essays and poems that won prizes.She is also interested in animals .

The Deserted Love

This is a fable poem of a Goddess who because of her eternal love became a Sunflower

The divine Goddess came down
To the earth far around
To see the qualities that ruled
In the land ,green and abound.

The Goddess roamed here and there
For many days dwelled on earth
But she lost her magic wand
So could not go back to her heavenly abode.

She felt lonely around
So as a company decided to make a Lord
From the power she had
To follow her around.

She collected the Sunrays
And decorated them with petals and dew
To creat a beautiful Lord
That shone with the light subdue.

She looked at the Lord she created
As bright,strong and handsome
And fell in love with him
Confessing her feelings with sweet words sum .

The Lord created smiled back
And the two roamed around

Between the apple trees dense
She-the lost one and He-her bright creation ,
together bound.

They played with the wind
And listened to melodies of breeze
Walking on the rainbow
Riding the thunder and breeze.

But soon that night came
When the sunlight that created the Lord ended.
So the Lord vanished with the setting Sun
No more visible in the darkness woven.

The Goddess searched him everywhere
And felt lonely in her attire
She wept bitter tears
And felt cold with despair.

She searched the Lord
But couldn't find him
She called the pale rainbow
She called the cruel wind .

They told her that the Lord
Had vanished in the dark
As the sunlight by which she had
created him
Was darkened by the night
aghast.

The Goddess then prayed
From her power again

She collected the Sunlight and dew
And created her beloved Lord again.

But the Lord did not recognize her
He however gave her a boon
That she could return back
To her abode divine.

The Goddess finally gave up
And returned to her abode high
But she could not forget her created Lord
And shed tears more than her worth.

Her eternal love took form
Of divine Sunflowers
That grew in the fields
With golden yellow color to shower.

We know that-
The Sunflower looks at the Sun
Smiling at the sunlight and dew
From which the created Lord had come
To become the Goddess's loved one.

Such is the eternal love
Of the Goddess and her created Lord
With the golden glow of Sunflowers
Beautified every moment by the sunlight created
Lord.
True love is eternal
And always beautiful one.

Maisyara Fazleen Haznie Binti Mohd Fauzi

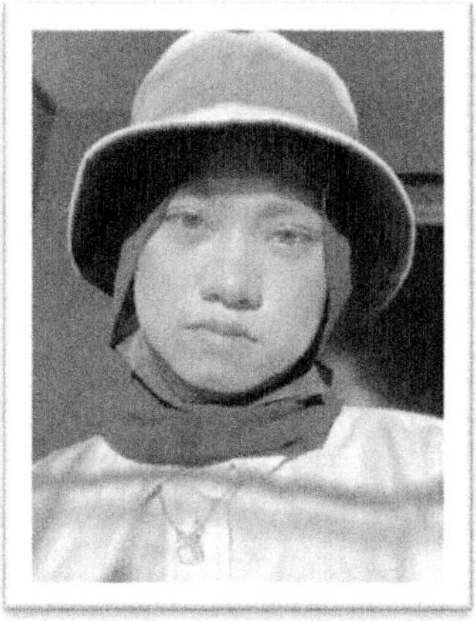

Maisyara as her pen name, Sarae is an August 1999 baby that was born in a small yet busy town of Rawang in Malaysia. She always has been dreaming of having her own poetry shown to the world. Writes her own novel since 15 years old guided her to be as what she are today, even she didn't have the chance to post of her novels anywhere yet. She never give up of writing her own thoughts as she adores the English Language very much.

You Are Home

I imagine
you are home.
The home that tends
to be as the best comfort,
The home that tends
to be as warm & calmness,
The home that tends
to finally be as a whole.
But what a pity;
You breached
till I bleed.
Thanks to you;
'Cause now all you seeing,
is the cold-blooded me.

I Still Thought About You

Day by day,
Months by months,
I still thought about
you every single time.
How powerful of you impacted my life,
From nothing
to everything.
I would bet on my
every single dime,
Just for you to notice;
That I'm waiting
for you,
Endlessly.

I Am the Catch

After some time,
I finally realised
about something.
I always chase people
and at the end,
they'd leave.
That's when I realised;
I'm done chasing people
who wasn't gonna see
my worth.
To chase no one,
And of course baby,
I am the catch.

Never Leave Me in (Misery)

Butterflies in the
blue sky,
Lavenders in
ample green field,
Oh one guy in voices
of husky,
Leaving beautiful scars
in millionhold,
In shooting stars
I wished risky,
For the name of
this counterworld,
I prayed for your honest;
To never leave me
in misery.

Matthew Alhassan Johnson

Matthew Lala Johnson better known by his pen name \"Jamaal\" is a Sierra Leonean Writer, Poet, Song-writer, Singer and Rapper... \"Jamaal\" is an acronym for the title; \"Just a man after a legacy\"

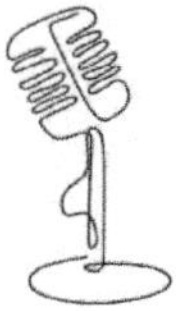

Depression

What\'s happening to me?
I find it hard to comprehend.
Is this the beginning of the end?
Is it the moment for the clouds to descend
And adopt me to the other world of no friend?

For I hardly find sleep on my bed..
Constantly, I hear strange voices in my head..
They\'re not helping me, instead,
They keep on tormenting me
And tempting me to turn stones into bread..

My state of mind is a mess like a white cloak
covered in stains..
I act as if I\'m good but deep down I\'m in pains..
For my body is free but my soul is locked up in
Chains..

Honestly I\'m hating it right here..
I\'m at the end of the tunnel but the light is not
even quite clear..
Why is my reality a Living nightmare?
A voice said to me; \"My Dear\"
\"All of these are the devil\'s Idea\"..

But I\'m weak, my wings are broken..
And I feel forsaken, like a slave
Abandoned in a Cave..

My mind is at war with itself..
I\'m now just a shadow of myself..
Depression has robbed me off my strength...

If I were a Poet

If I were a poet...
I\'ll take poetry out on a date
In a garden...
I\'ll make her a bone of my bone and a flesh of my flesh...
I\'ll be Adam and poetry will be Eve...
Even if she lures me into sin
And make me eat of the forbidden fruit,
Her side I will never leave..
I\'ll follow her to every path,
I\'ll build her a special place in my heart...

If I were a poet...
I\'ll take poetry for a dance on the moon,
And then we\'ll create a kingdom in the universe...
I\'ll be her King and her, my Queen,
Together we\'ll rule the universe...
Planets and Galaxies shall bow to our throne...

If I were a poet...
Evil will flee to a hiding space...
The world will be a peaceful place
Free from wickedness..
As I\'ll fill the world with words of love and goodness
Towards one another...

If I were a poet
Changing lives with words will be my duty...

I\'ll let the world see why Poetry is such a beauty
To behold and cherish like pure gold...

If I were a poet...
I am sure...
When I\'m sick poetry will be my cure...
It\'ll make my soul so clean and pure...
My life will be so complete...

Md.Mahabubur Rahman

Md.Mahabubur Rahman,he,who born Abhaoa office road,Bhola,Bangladesh.From very childhood he is a nature lover and have great fascination on God and His creation.He did his graduation in Bio-Chemistry and Molecular Biology from Rajshahi University,Bangladesh.

Mr.Mahabubur Rahman joined as pharmaceutical chemist(QC.Analyst) at Aristopharma Limited,Dhaka, and next at Renata Limited(Formarly Pfizer Ltd) as senior executive.He is the founder of 'Joynal Foundation'-a Charitable organization for deprived.As a poet he published his first poetry publication,32-er Bankae(৩২-এর বাঁকে) at February,2019.

God's Mercy & Love

What a moonlight night! The eastern sky was loon.
We been changed, God! But not You and the Moon.

It was a sunny noon, in the field I was feeling burn,
God, we fired ourselves, but not by You and the Sun.

It was just dawn; I was then feeling reddish bright.
God, we shadowed one other but not You and the Light.

In the forest, we walked together and breathed in pair, God, we strangled one another, but not by You and the Air.

That was a football match; both the team had separate jersey,

God, today humanity dressed differently, but not You & Your mercy.

It was a lawn, dew's glitters like pearl, on green mass, God, we been rough in surface but not You and the Grass.

What a lovely livable basement! Where we all living stand!

God, we grabbed the nature but not by You and your Land.

It's going a jealousy game, where we ourselves pollutes and rub,

God, You the God of sand & soul, having no change in mercy & Love.

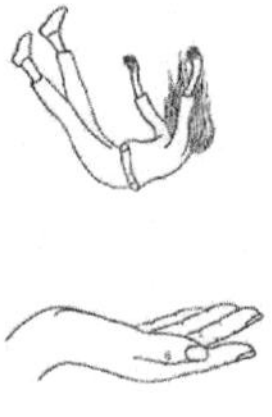

Child's pain of Divorced parents

Mom, I'm by your womb, with your bone ,blood and skull,
My pain similar like a high hill, how could do I make it null.

Dad, I'm your drop of love, with your gene, genera & hidden bee,
My tears formed Icy mountain, which flows like murmur sea.

Mom I'm your protected soul, nurtured by your soft, lips and palm,
My heart boils like molten lava, who will touch to make me calm.

Dad you were my shelter, like two strong hand closed nest,
Your separation tore me two halves, froze me like a frozen chest.

Mom, I was your childhood guitar, who read your hidden mind,
Why God make them parent? Who are selfish and unkind?

Dad, I was your first follower, followed your breaking tone,
Why God make them parent? Who, two build a, fragile cone!

Mom, I was your breath of love, petals enclosed ovaries egg,
Love me ,My right! Why for your love will I beg?

Dad, I was your sea of love, fluid enclosed enriched arm,
Love me ,my right, Don't treat me like a terrible germ!

Parents, I was your fruits of love, in your emotional golden time.
Why you two roasted me alive, making me a lifeless chime?

Parents, I am your combined soul, will move you and you build way,
Why you changed me and my green life, turning me as milk to w

MD Mahedi Hassan Rony

I believe that man can't do anything without willing of God. The creativity of mine of poem is given by God. So I pay all the gratitude to God for my creative knowledge. And Beg from him so that I can give u you more good deed.

My Life

The sun has risen.

My ride has begun.

I don’t know riding.

So I am very fearing.

A few times I am driving.

Slightly I am learning.

Thus I am riding.

I am facing some turnings.

Some time I am slipping.

Some time I am paining.

And the situations I am overcoming.

I am going through my riding.

Some time I am speedy.

Some time I am static.

But never forever,

Again I am moving.

Some experience I am getting.

My ripeness is increasing.

In my journey,

I am noticing one thing.

Some time I Spring is coming.

Sometime Spring is going.

In wishing Spring again,

Patience is an important thing.

However in this playing.

I am forgetting that

my pathway is minimizing.

Now I am thinking,

what have been gained from the riding.

In the evening,

my destination is appearing

The sun is setting.

My journey is at just ending.

The sun has set.

My life story has closed.

I am waiting for a New

I am waiting for a new

I hope from my deep

God will show me an wonderful view

I am waiting for a new

When the dyed river will overflow

And will get its momentum

I am waiting for a new

When the drought will go

It will Appear the rainfall

I waiting for a new

When the chippy plants will grow

They will vitalize totally

I am waiting for a new

When the night will be turned

the sun will sparkle on the day

I am waiting for a new

When my all attempt will avail my destiny will smile on me

I am waiting for a new

When my dream will come true

I will grope it in my live

So I never give up my hope

Loser

I am minute loser of mind
Loser loser loser
saying this mentally
I just control my agony
I am not loser worldly
It's just trucks of mind governing way of inferiority
loser loser loser
It's just a word of dictionary
I use it in my life properly
Saying loser to criticize me
I take it as positive body
And acute to my superiority

Mukut Borpujari

Mukut Borpujari was born on 25th December, 1989, in jorhat, Assam. He graduated with major in English Literature from Arya Vidyapeeth College, Guwahati, and completed his Masters in Computer Application (MCA) in 2015, from Guru Ghasidas Central University, Bilaspur, CG.He started writing poems and articles when he was still in college, and his early poems were published in various local newspapers and megazines. His other hobbies and interests include Computers & Internet, Playing Cricket, Listening to Music and Reading.

Untitled

In to the dream you came,
And across the length of
My windswept room,
You trod with a lighter tread,
To bring sleep to my drooping eyelids...

On Defense of Poetry

Last night I have given up on poetry,
As you have suggested
Once so many years ago.
Even then you knew,
Prosperity would have no quarrel,
You said, with a man who reads the paper,
Drinks tea, goes shopping on Sundays,
And lets anger be general
In the household;
Your raspy voice resounded eerily in the hollow room,
In the hollow room? Why??
...I hate to state an abstract thing.

A New Dawn

Far upon the distant skies,
Always gazing into our hearts –
We are the darkness and we are the light.
For, we are the glitter of the stars.
Bring forth the shores of the sun,
Living out from the shadows of the dark.
For, we are the light and darkness together.
From stars light reflect back into our hearts.
Through this world that we live,
An ocean rising and falling deep within,
A sparkle of light in our eyes,
Mirrored as a veil of stars in the sky.
Here we find our voices rhyme.
In the vast ocean of time,
In all of that we feel and see,
Is a new dawn that is about to unfold.
As we try to guide each other across,
To reveal the things that had been lost,
Our feelings unique in a natural way,
A vision of light comes to our reflections...

Evening

By memories

Of the days gone by,

In my solitude

You taunt me,

With memories that would

Never die;

I sit in my chair

Filled with despair,

There's no one more sad

As I sit and stare –

Gloom descending everywhere

At dusk...

Nadjeb Baud Pinote

Nadjeb B. Pinote is a 18 years old student from Mindanao State University-UTC . He is a senior high student and graduated as valedictorian when he was in elementary. He is the 3rd son of Mrs. Sairah Azis and Mr. Alde Pinote. He loves writing poem, poetry and story. Because of his amazing skills in all fields he received many awards at school and in every Competition. He is a self-motivated and reliable person who is pursuing his dreams. He wants to be a famous and successful writer to share his wisdom through emotions. Soon he will be what he capable of becoming.

"Journey"

Life is a journey
To live with a purpose is necessary
But to live in
scarcity is uneasy;
Facing life's trial is not infinity
To give up in the battle is not a dignity;
Indeed, it's an ignominy.
But to face the life's challenges is the best way
To achieve dreams and victory.

To have feathers in cap is not a majority;
But to achieve your life's ambition is your priority!
Because you deserve to live successfully;
Not to live; melancholy...
No matter what life's taste or palatability
Whether it's crummy nor creamy;
Even you don't like its savory;
Just go with its flow; calmly
I'm sure you can do it perfectly;
So, don't you doubt to attain the trophy.

To live your dreams is not your option
Because it is your obligation.
You need be an inspiration
And be the good conclusion
For the next generation;

But before that, don't forget my prescription!
My Dear...
Whatever Will be your destination
Don't forget your origination

Don't get drowned by your perfection
Because that's not the right direction
To obtain your final destination.

Dear... Always remember this quotation
" Success is not a destination
But it is just a part of journey ".....

Sooner the Sun will Rise

Life is hard
And don't be sad.
Don't you make things bad
In Every time you got mad.
Life is as sticky as dirty mud
Don't be coward!
Don't be morbid!
Don't be afraid...
Just go and hold..
You need to be bold!
And pretend you're glad!
For the fortune you had!

Did you forgot what they told?
For you is to embolden your hardihood.
You're not as weak as unsound liquid
So don't get drowned with the viscid mud.

Did you forgot what you dreamed?
For you is to awake from your nightmarish dream.
You're not as strong as a wood
But tougher than a solid gold.
Don't say "I can't" instead say" I should!!."

In your strength I believed.
For what you've done, I accepted
At least you fought in a battle and never yield.
Unlike you stepped with the Japanese barefooted.
Who colonized our dear land?

Strengthen your wings
Put back your Zest
Open your eyes
And pave for your fresh life's pace.
Insha'Allah!! Sun will rise...

When you're about to...

When you're about to go
And someone blocks the flow
You really want to grow
But there's no wind to be blow

When you really want to draw
The life of arts you woo
But someone stopped you,
A words woefully say " Don't show "!

You truly won't withdraw,
But you're scared from sorrow
You're probably want to plow
But you're afraid if they would say
" you're Really Slow "!

When you're gonna make things possible
And someone whispers; “It’s Impossible "
You want to make rules Permissible
But you're not compatible.

You really want to hold
But you're not yet bold
You really want to mold the ball
But it was fixedly untouchable

Surely, to them you don't have a way
Even You blew them away
Oh! “It’s a cooking show "! Probably
That would they say

Yet, things were not easy
Especially when you're not on their priority
"You're such a messy scratch"!
that what they see

Sooner you'll live successfully
Just make your own way
Keep going on your journey
And work to obtain your destiny

Nahid Nigar Ansari

Nahid Nigar Ansari (Naaz) lives in Kanpur, Uttar Pradesh. Recently, she got a new interest in writing poems from her friend. She loves to learn new things and still learning. "If they can do it then why I can't" she thinks like that and because of her this strong mindset she has learn a lot. She is a huge fan of Korean drama and likes to listen k-pop because of BTS. She wants to make herself unique and loving.

Fake Love

You were just standing there
I was roaming around here and there
For you to just look at me
I once thought you could be
Because there were millions of eyes
How could you see my heart cries
I was innocent that's why i got swayed
On that very moment i got preyed
You just wanted to play with me
From this uncanny feeling please let me free
For me this new thing was mystery
I want to delete our history
I thought I am a protagonist
You were just my feeling's antagonist
My life was empty paper, in it i wrote this script
Only a thought of what i did, my heart ripped
I want to ease my mind
That's why i am being kind
I don't want this to be my destiny
My life can't be this funny
I set you free, when you said
My memories starting to get fade
I started a new life without you
Life was this beautiful, I never
knew
Now, I am free from that
handcuff
Called Fake love, Fake love,
Fake love.

Nigel Mark Edward

Hi, my name is Nigel. I enjoy reading playing chess and going for long walks.

What on Earth?!

Can remember what that man said, want him to be dead.
Keeps calling me a little boy, he thinks he's playing with a toy.
Going to treat him like a fool, just a tool.
What on earth has he been saying.
Not playing.

T.V. all day

Such a useless lump of dead weight, full of hate.
He does nothing but sit there all day with nothing to say.
A man without a wife, a man without a life.
Just couldn't live my life that way watching T.V. all day.
When I listen to his stupid words, that man doesn't even understand the bees and the birds.
Just sitting in his chair all day, how could anyone live there life that way.

Betrayed

My heart feels broken, remembering the words you have spoken.
Echoing around and around and around again.
Don't want to remember, as sweet as sweet can be.
The words you said to said to me, forever and ever.
The last thing you said, I can't get out of my head.
Don't care if I'm gone, you make me feel like I don't belong.
Feeling cold inside, my feelings I cannot hide.
I know every day I will feel this way.
Just one more thing I want to say, the love I have for you is not a game.
You think you can have fun and play.
What you have stolen, will always feel betrayed.

Cloven hoof

People treat me as if I walk around with a cloven hoof, what they say is not the truth.
They always say who have I hit, they sound like they mean it.
Telling me I am going to be tamed, is insane.
Such a stupid use of language, what is wrong with the people of Cambridge?

Self Esteem

Sitting around, bored out of my brains is always the same, is making me insane.

Looking out of the window, they are people I don't know. Don't know where to go, what to do,

I just don't know. If I was big and strong, and felt like I could belong.

Can't shake this sadness out of my head, Nobody would care if I was dead.

Don't know what to do, people treat me like I have no clue.

Little Boy

He keeps on calling me a little boy, Think he is playing with a toy.

Going to lose my temper, every word I can remember.

Want to tear him apart, going to start. He doesn't ever have a heart.

Njabulo Magubane

I like creative writing and autography. I an extrovert person I like being around people and also music. I've always liked poetry, it keeps me alive.

The Unfurling Of Love

To love someone is nothing
To be loved by someone is something
But to be loved by the person you love is everything,
It enjoyable

To enjoy love
Date someone who is willing to share your pain and joy
Someone that it is easy to understand
Be with someone who will go extra miles for you

Love and take care of them
Don't try to change them
Rather love and accept them for who they are

Trust, loyalty and patience
Keeps the relationship alive and strong
Never let of the one you love
Keep trying until everything falls into place

We live half remembered dreams
Until we meet the one who changes everything
If you find that person
Make them your eternity
Don't let the pain of separation wound you

Nkosna Dlibani Jwara Ngomane

He is an upcoming poet from South African.

Born as Nkosana Dlibani Jwara Ngomane.

Known as Nkobla.J - The poet.

You could search/follow & like him on facebook.

Nkobla.J is a dreamer, who has a dream to publish his own poetry books.

A smile

I just want a smile
A smile can buy the world
Plus with your beauty
A smile goes a long way
You don't have to show me
You don't have to give it to me
All I want is just a smile
Your smile dear

A smile can
change the world
A smile can
touch a stranger
A smile can
make one feel warm
A smile can
say a thousand words
So please not for me
But for your own good
Can I have your smile

Still

I still
She still
We still

We do many things still
& yes our love is made of steel
We like keeping our love still
& yes we also do steal
But we never stand still
cause time never stand still

Still water runs deep
So we keep our love still
So that it runs deep as well

I still
She still
We still

Time isn't standing still
So we move with the times
So that our love never stand still

We also do steal
good ideas from places
Then we steal
best ideas from partners
So our love can burn still

I still
She still
We still

There are little things we do still
We friends still
There are little things we do keep still
We talk still
There are little things we change still
We fight still

But I still
& She still
Then We still

We make our love strong still
by thinking for each other still
We keep our fire burning still
by loving each other still
We get along still
by connecting with each other still

I still
She still
We still

Our love is made of steel
so our hearts are strong
For our love we do steal
so our dream lives strong
Our love is kept very still
although we never stand still

I still
She still
We still

Pramod Kumar BS

Animal lover, listening music.

Two Soulless Bodies

She was missing something in her life
As he was searching something in his life,
And the way both met ... you can call it an accident, or a miracle or a destiny.
And it's all started when he tried to wipe the tears on her eyes when he saw her for the first time.
A flower started blooming on his heart after many years, when she slept on his shoulder.
They were not talking, but their memories were.
And they both connected with bond called pain
Two soulless bodies were comforting each other!
As people says 'When two broken hearts meet, they find their missing part in each other'.

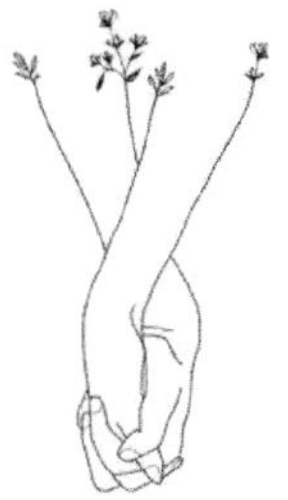

Pratik Gupta

An Engineer turned Poet sounds cliché but I've been breaking stereotypes long before I could even spell them.
Every man has set out to be someone with his aspirations, but I've been searching for more than that, somewhere I belong. And throughout this journey, my writings, my words are my greatest ally.
To sum it up, I'm an avid reader, a cricket player and enthusiast, and a hopeless romantic.

Darkness

Darkness scares me sometimes
The burning sun, the blinding LEDs
They lights are so bright that they obscure my face.
You can't see well when it's too bright
You squint just a bit.
Maybe I think of happiness as this
I can't comprehend life as well.

In my darkness, I am close
Huddled with arms around my knees
Not blinded, not fiery
Just me and the dimness of reality.
And in the dark,
I see myself.....
Clear at last...!

My Earnest Manifestation.

The clock's ticking and is already in ambush.
Confined into an immortal bliss.
Fetch it or let it sway away
For it only gnaws at those who stick.
Ruptured at ends or in between
Gasping in a hollow shaft
Epitome of my earnest manifestations
Swindled by worldly craft.

I only see you!

You aren't mine, but sometimes
When a cruel breeze of reminisce passes through,
I can't defy , but I only see you .
On the back of the mind where my fantasy lives,
You are out there somewhere, and that's still a bliss.
Because all I can reckon, I asked you to be classy
You aren't mine, but sometimes,
I hope you are happy.

And I step out again.

When I took my first step out of home

I pretended I had a world to conquer.

Cities to leave a footprint on

Countries to rummage into

I wanted to be a chameleon

Losing who I was as I go ahead

Changing who I am as I step right in

Yet I carried I didn't shed.

Every story I walked left it's story with me

Every sigh told me its deep secrets.

I was alien and known

I knew too much but I didn't know enough.

I have many homes yet I wander

Or maybe I am desperate for one I don't know.

Wanderlust is a bold faced lie

A lust for walking into darkened rooms

On empty story lanes

A lust for staring at your bed at night

Knowing it will forget you soon.

Wanderlust is a bold faced lie

Some wanderers have no way to go

Some lusters just want a cozy night

So I, step out again

Rajinder Kaur

Rajinder Kaur (Rashu), born on 01.01.1981 is daughter of Krishan Singh and Harbhajan Kaur and is married to Gurpreet Singh. She presently resides in Amritsar, Punjab. She is a B.com graduate. Her hobbies are poetry and drawing. She has written 3 Poetry books i.e., ambrosial aita (English), Meri kavy vidhaye (Hindi) and Chand haritima (Hindi).

Liars

Liars with a great sense of acting
A selfish with a lower image of creativity
Can cheat the poor little lovable hearts.
My dear friend life is not a liar's tart.
Liar is ready to deceive himself
For the cheater gets inferiority for thyself
Esteemed in low grade personality
Holds his head high in imagination for his
criminality.
Don't just betray your emotions
Liar just backstabs his solutions
Live a king-size life
Love yourself and always thrive .

You or me

Me before you or you before me.
Following a constant pattern.
Life starts from mother's womb.
And ends at Mother Earth's bed.
Earth is round
Thunder storm and hurricanes swirl in search
So as day follows night and vice versa
Sun is round, moon too shows a circular start.
Parents have children at their response
Grownups have parents to take care
So the "me before you and you before me "goes on
Life has a set pattern
Nature shows minutely with little lantern
What you give you get in turn.
God is the soul creator.
Deeds are the soul destroyer.
So as "Me before you or you before me."

Scenario of seasons

Seasons come and give excitement.
For every change there is an arrangement.

Some bring love, laugh flowers and bloom.
Others store ice, rain pouring and leaves doom.

Seasons are part of life
Dawn changes to dusk with every drive.

Hibernation, migration and harvesting.
All occur due to earth's rotating.

Human beings understand season's scenario.
Birds and animals do respond to earth's imperio.

Change with every turn is must.
Live a life of love and lust.

Nostalgia

In the busy schedules of our life
Sometimes loneliness creeps and cuts you like a knife
Sweet and sour memories keep on covering
Life starts to recollect all those rememberings
The childhood stands at the threshold
Young age with sweet smelling fold
Nostalgic the way one becomes
All emotions occur in front of a dumb
You just can't speak
Feelings are at their peak
Life is at reminisce
Presence is allowed to dismiss
Youthful love starts hurting
Innocent aggravation recalls your cheating.
Cunning beautiful thoughts pinch
All your bitter emotions fly like a finch
Memories keep on coming
Breath wants that sigh with a sitting
All that's over stays connected
Life lived should always be respected.

Renu Pohani

Professionally, Renu is Business Director with more than 24 plus years in managing global teams in the IT industry. She is also a mother to a young, beautiful and very creative girl. Her other interests include adventure sports, road excursions, traveling, and cooking. She has a passion for writing and she writes from her heart. She seeks to build a connection with her readers and touch them by sharing her life stories of breakthrough moments, of hard work, of struggles, of failures, of how she crossed the threshold from darkness to light. Her consolidated writings can be scanned on her webpage:
https://rpohani.wixsite.com/koshernod

Bring It On

Hey there, you gotta think harder, that's not me with whom you can falter,

Nothing today can sway me or alter. Me here getting stronger and bold,

Bring it on, my endurance you gotta behold.

You gotta be the hardest to put the brawl, Be aware of the might I carry to still crawl,

Away from sarcasm, from shrewdness, from all scorn. I have risen above and much beyond I hold,

Bring it on, my endurance you gotta behold.

You gotta try with all in your stride, I am unshaken and much beyond I rise,

Of your petty games I do not compromise. I have brushed too much count under the sturdiest fold,

Bring it on, my endurance you gotta behold.

You hurl the pernicious prose to me to tear, Ah! they seem paltry to instill the fear,

Sadly the stupor only casts your despair. I am on the strong ground and I have cast a mould,

Bring it on, my endurance you gotta behold.

You might be too big or on count be many, Try the meanest rollick or be as uncanny,

I fare to mock the deceitful myriads be that any. I reckon the courage to stand alone uncaged, unsold

Bring it on, my endurance you gotta behold.

Disparage, mockery, artifice and scorning deeds,
Have never had and have nothing to heed,

Hatching and deception will never own the seal.
Gentleness, purity and loyalty are mightily priced and till date unsold

Bring it on, my endurance you gotta behold.

Courage, confidence, self-worth and purity, I engrave Respect, resilience, gratitude and humility I crave,

I reap only my thoughts and actions, and will carry it to the grave.

Of thriving, struggles and accolades I have many stories untold,

Bring it on, my endurance you gotta behold.

Yeah, we have met…

Yeah we met, in my four plus decades we
somewhere met...

Here and there, off n on, on so many tracks we met.
Each one met to play his/ her part in my fable,

And each one gave me a vision and made me able.
Light I call gave me 'wisdom', 'sanity' and made me
'versed',

A beam to equip me to be enlightened and surged,
Of just not the mere superficiality but to the core,

Made me go astute and proceed ahead much
assured. Each one of you gave me a new persona to
beam,

Some made me compassionate while some turned
me gleam, while some embraced me with their
warmth,

Some showed their true self under the shroud.
Some hugged me with pure selfless unadulterated
love,

Some made me wiser to judge the stench in the
verbose; some also blandished me with pernicious
prose,

Whereas some groomed me to sparkle and beam in the cove. Some tried to butt me to the murky abysmal fall,

Some enjoyed the glory in the gratuitous call. Ah! Little did they know they consorted in sequel,

A ferocious prudent me with an even bigger stall. Such small were their musings to rend some down,

Little they had to do, to prove them clown. Remember that understated past can't escape the inevitable judge,

From your own karmas none can ever nudge. Mocks and scratches only polished and groomed,

Adversities only uttered the beginning of a distinct bloom. Much sanguine, tenacious and prudent after the tour,

I bloomed radiant, energetic, and veracious in a new contour. Angelic were some, who cuddled me in my lowest lows,

Those that bore no connection to the blood flow. Made and earned their glorious self a more human course,

In the vast sea of venal, so rich and pious is their soul. Lest the darkness prevailed and drowned the kind,

These few scorched to fight the depraved mind, with humanity and fervor playing the mightiest might...

And they are reverberating in their true glorious fight. In their fight for humanity, goodness and brethren to prevail,

In the drowning expanse there's a hope for the sail....Love is powerful, mightier, bigger than the infamy swords,

What triumphs in the end is "what fosters the human chords."

Samson Oluyide

He is Samson Oluyide, a young writer who at first didn't see anything good concerning poetry. Until recently with the help of friends and family he saw the world of poetry and fell in love with it.
Now he has written poems and stories of different genre.

Monster at Mercy

I strive towards the future, in search of a savior,
the one thing I must change is my own bad
behavior.
The monster in the mirror; looking back at me,
is not the person I want the society to see.

All of my good times were nothing but a lie,
on my road to self-destruction, i was willing to die.
I cannot exchange all the mistakes that I have
made,
for the damage is done, and my bed has been made.

I have been through the hell, I have been through
the pain,
what is important to me now, my sobriety I desire.
Now I must face my own demons; change for
myself, family, and friends,
which now i am challenged with, in making
amends.

I pray for their forgiveness, at the end of my mercy,
I will conquer my demons, in my fight to be free.
I will prove to myself, and everyone I know,
That my life is a new game, and I'm in charge of the
show!!!

Self-love

I do not need your recognition.
I do not need your love.
I am fine on my own.
I just need self-love.

I have no pity or shame.
Even though I have been through so pain.
I am searching my soul.
I am rekindling my flame.

Meditating my mind.
Releasing these negative vibes.
To the mountains I climb.
It is my spiritual high name.

This course is charted.
My ship has set its course.
To the ones who are heartbroken.
Self-love is the cure.

There comes a time

There comes a time when you feel so alone
That moment when you feel so empty deep down your soul
But look at the bright side, you'll never feel so blue
You just have to be happy and joyful, and be grateful too

There comes a time when you feel everyone's so distant
Then you'll start asking yourself was I not that important?
But they are just there, it's just hard for you to communicate
Reach out to them it's never too late

There comes a time when you feel so insecure
You'll start doubting yourself, everything seems unsure
But the truth is, you just keep on overthinking and worrying about nothing
You are beautiful and worthy, coz babe you are something

There comes a time when you feel so hopeless
You think the world is unkind, everything you do is useless
But look around you, and see how nice this life could be
You just need to find your own happiness, someday you'll see.

Introvert II

I'm a typical person
Who loves to be alone
I can stay in my room all day long
I was like this all along
Friends? I only have few of them
But I'm glad even how a small group it has been
Cause I have a hard time communicating
I found it hard to express what I'm feeling

I'm not that comfortable with other people
Having visitors in the house for example
It's not that I don't like them coming around
It's just that I don't feel like having so much crowd

You can consider me as a shy type person
And I don't like to get too much attention
I hate it when I'm the center of attraction
It felt like I'm hyperventilating and in so much humiliation

I love to be in a secluded place
Avoiding so much noise and people's gaze
I also love to hear music
It makes me feel relaxed and less problematic

Being and introvert is also difficult
You will be less sociable as a result
But I know that one day I'll be that outgoing and friendly
Thanks for those who stays and understands me

Sean Tru Giovanni

Amir Tru is an American Muslim who grew up in poverty in a violent neighborhood. During his time in prison he fell in love with education, knowledge, communication and writing. You can find his writing with the hashtag #poetrybytru". He signs everything off with
Empower & Inspire…

Lyfe

Life is a dream on the way to death
Nothing more.. nothing less
Behind life's illusion.. it's the reality of death
In a conscious state.. beyond fear & regret
In it we are eternally blessed
Immortality.. how else can we exist?
The laws of nature, how can we resist?
This is eternal love and bliss-or- lows in an abyss..
All in the way you interpret it...
To deny God, is to deny existence. This is called stupidity and not ignorance..
Still feeble minds try to contradict with irrational resistance..
I AM eternal & God conscious.
I AM beyond the dream and the reality..
In both I co-exist..
Always, forever and eternally
I exist

Shireesha M V

A girl named Miss. Shireesha M V is the daughter of Mr.Venkataravana Reddy and Mrs. Ashwathamma. She is from Mudhalahalli(village), Chikkaballapur (Dist.). Her writings are reflection of her thoughts. She feels her presence at the fullest in her writings. Right now she is pursuing B.Sc. in BMS College for Women - Bangalore. She is passionate about writing poems, stories, micro fables in Kannada and English.
She is willing to thank the pioneers for her motivation to be a writer. He is her Hindi teacher, Mr. Athikulla, and also her sisters.

Instagram id: our_blur_image
Mail id: kanna1752019@gmail.com"Be, learner, be guider"

To sculpt

Praying for sunrise,
to make it laugh.
Kneeling for sunrise,
to vain her foam.
Wishing for sunrise,
to shine smile.

Hair is wet,
but,
faith it's mate.
As pure soul,
never squeezed,
never stabbed.

Gravity acts
to, white space.
Vibrant, ignorant
are in duet.
Ideology shrinked,
everything swirls.

Hope for sunrise,
to pour ,
to sculpt,
will be history,
let it be history,
with colored words.

Floral makeup

Language of my night knows,
colors of my chores,
possibilities at doorsteps.
As well as,
insecurities for my nap,
barriers of my eyesight

It Assembles my actions,
summons my feelings,
pileup my practices,
trains my mind,
to the sun smiles.
It knows me well.

It's a door to dream song,
mentor of my chores.
It make elegant floral makeup,
to make myself fruity,
it's a magic of self-love.
Jewel of "Be Thyself".

Adore

Adore your chores,
it's a celebration of your decisions.
Adore your mates,
it's the magic of your acceptance.
Adore to truth,
it's the trust of victory.
Adore to failures,
it's faith in your efforts.
But,
Adoring yourself,
is an honor to yourself.

Sowjanya M

Sowjanya M is an I.T. professional and lives in Bengaluru. She is passionate about writing and her penchant for writing has helped voice her opinions by writing blogs on various topics and views in her blog site.

The Walls were High

Yes, there was a garden and the walls were high..
You are the bright sun of life
Who smiles like a bright day
Whose eyes are so deep like a calm ocean

A view of you reminds of the morning dew
Your presence is like a gentle breeze
Your words are like soothing music

You are there regardless of the changing seasons
You are valued loved and cared for many reasons
You are the only one the eyes searches for amidst many persons

Yes, there was a garden and the walls were high..
The walls of the fort were built so high
That neighing horses and strongest forces had to sigh
You dint mean to stop by but you did and left without a goodbye

Sunita Nanda

She is Sunita Nanda, a senior software engineer working in IT.

She is also an Author, Blogger, Artist and Loves Singing, Dancing, travelling and making friends.

She believes in positive attitude.

The Day I met You

Your soft warm hands
Touching my head
Your sweet innocent smile
making me go chirpy
Your altruistic love
fortunate to have you in this world
your pure solicitude
I feel so lucky and grateful
Often i wonder is there true love exist
your presence in my life answers to it
I believe there cannot be any feelings
Which can describe a mothers love unending
True love is not always about a guy and a girl
true love for me resides in my mother's heart

Syeda Deena Yousaf

Deena is simple and introvert guy being silent she speaks through her words, prefers long walks in company of nature .

She is book lover and she can steal books also, Ha-ha.

Lover of beauty, painting and art.

Harvest…

The paltry efforts of my pen,

Are to graze in every swath or belt,

Thoughts are weird, mingled still to comb,

Ear! Never heard the cosmic bells of love.

The dictions are not part of any folder,

Resounding, uncouth upon thy shoulder,

Now are spurting, cracking its hides,

Will find scathing notions of chide.

Hey!!! Virgin seek a lonely place,

That Child is going to bear and face,

Seek somewhere across the bay,

Thine pipes will on the cliffs.

Find somewhere behind the hills,

Hey! Child of Mediterranean! Find those rills.

The newly born child of my pen,

Have to seek an abyss den.

The Castle...

Untie my lips' knots,

Let them set free those,

Words which never uttered or flee,

Be my heart's notes.

Let's brim to brim in cohesion,

All mine realms in yours possession,

Take my heart in humble siege,

All the berserk warriors standing

In yours humble prestige.

The Bleak Corner.

Coiled and composed over the nook,
With thousands of stories in eyes,
Roaming souls, piercing glance as rook,
Ever cupped my hands ever looked at skies.
O' profoundest Dale make my groans' echo,
Mine pounding chest, let it be heard,
The untold tales had beyond the ego,
Have succumbed sighs for softer heart
The medley is composed in pain as fate,
Marching souls with jingles as infidels,
With frown, never speak just kill and hate,
Since ages youth finds life nothing but riddles.
Yes!! Drenched soil in blood and sweat,
Kneaded my frame, seeds have been sown,
The buds bloom even better in threat ,
Eager hearts and eager pacing are to born.

Tahoor Hamid Rathore

Tahoor Hamid Rathore was born and raised in Kashmir, in the beautiful mountain state of India.
Tahoor considers her faith and family to be most important to her. If she isn't spending time with her family and friends you can always find her wandering through words. A civil Engineer by profession loves to traipse through words whenever she gets time to write.
Thank you all!

Her Forbidden Love

She was all alone in her journey of love
Keep on healing on her own
His face was pestered on her mind
And she unintentionally made every time herself a fool
She only wanted herself to be loved by him
And he hated her whole existence like a dupe
She was a lonely wanderer in this soul crushing journey
Trapped in melancholy of love not wanting to soothe

Life (An unpredicted journey)

Reverie of emotions scintillating my soul
Making me ponder on life amidst groan
Some proved to be an ultimate soul healer
And some proved only an ephemeral shone
Some proved alluringly captivating to my eyes
And some were pestered on my mind like a frown
Unwinding those twisty roads of surprises
Tantalizing off my burdened ratty soul
In this unpredicted critical journey of life
Colors keep on yondering away like a yon

My Dad my superhero

O My Dear precious Adored father!
O My Dear Eternal love!
Only you are my orbs color from white to silver
Only you are my profound pain healer
O My Dear precious Adored father!
O My Dear Eternal love!
Relentless love of yours for me
Arduously sets my tired soul free
O My Dear precious Adored father!
O My Dear Eternal love!
Ever smiling face of yours
Unruffled back all my fears
O My Dear precious Adored father!
O My Dear Eternal love!
All I want is to drape around your arms
All I want is to desorb away your frowns
O My Dear precious Adored father!
O My Dear Eternal love!
I am at peace, my souls at rest
For with your love I am so blessed
O My Dear precious Adored father!
O My Dear Eternal love!
Thank you Dad for being an eventual soul healer
Thank you Dad for being an ultimate epitome of concealer

A Broken Soul

And in my own being shining like a star,
The soul unknowingly filled with a treacherous scar,
Tried to be her best yet deep down moaning her flaws,
Still she in her inner self indulging in some beautiful dreams!

Tanushree Das Ghosh

Brought up in the beautiful valley of Dehradun, Tanushree did her schooling as well as Masters in English and has always felt connected to poetry and fiction. She writes poems under the pseudonym Taruchaya. Post marriage, she resides in Kolkata. Poetry writing is her means of expressing unsaid thoughts and feelings. Inspired by Nature, she tries to find beauty in little things and joys in passing moments. She has been writing poems since the age of eleven. You can read her poems at: taruchaya.wordpress.com or simply search taru.chaya at Instagram.

Rainbow Reflection

The prism of tiny raindrops
made two colorful arcs.
A bridge over another develops
between four defined marks.
A carefree bird flew across
and got drenched in colour.
Alas, neither rainbows can emboss
nor do they meet each other.
Somewhere far in the horizon,
they connect the sky and earth.
Like lovers who sigh and yearn,
while the world laughs with mirth.
The double rainbows slowly fade
and vanish just as they suddenly came.
Had the rainbows stubbornly stayed,
would we love them just the same?

My Father's Red Wet Shoes

These late night thundershowers...
when rain simply overpowers,
leaves puddles of disappointment
and cleaning after as a punishment.
Amidst the wet mess I stopped to see,
my father's shoes wet with melancholy.
He daily wears those canvas red shoes,
though they had worn out of use.
I tried to put one foot in -
it fell short yet felt akin.
I wanted to walk on my father's shoes,
but his responsibilities are too huge.
Maybe in the future I shall find my way,
to make him proud of me someday.
No matter the outcome...**even** if I lose,
I'll try to fit in my father's red wet shoes!

The Nocturnal Spirit

When the stars slumber quietly
and the crickets sing lullabies,
I sit up on the edge of the bed
staring at the trespassing light
from the street lamp outside.
The bright light cannot penetrate me.
I thought I was an apparition
wandering in search of a lost friend.
As I looked to my right -
there she was...

A faceless shadow on the wall
staring back at me
Was she who I've been searching for...
the nocturnal spirit sitting alone?
Since the darkness covered the clock,
only the tick tock could be heard
along with the drag of the ceiling fan.
As an instinct to feel proximity,
I raised my hand ...
she did the same.

But what I touched was merely a shadow,
just the way she gives me company
often on a lonely long night
When my shadow stays by my side,
I'm wide awake but never alone...
While the world blissfully sleeps...
caressed by the satin breeze,
I still sit at the edge of the bed

staring at the trespassing light
from the street lamp outside!

Taurai Zulu

Taurai zulu, who is popularly known in the public domain as Guru poet. He was born in 1997 in Zambia

In 2018 he completed his high school diploma currently, he is a student at Malcolm Moffat College of education pursuing his diploma in mathematics and Physical Education (PE).At the age 19 he firmly started to use his ability to write director both drama and poetry which he was given a first chance to direct poetry in 2015. He was awarded his first certificate as a best male recitor poetry category .in 2020 got another certificate as a best-spoken word poet at chawama arts festival

Dear Sky (based on true story)

Dear sky...
I know I\'m just a boy
But I still look towards the shooting stars
To become like Akon, a pop star

Like the oceans, I flow to and fro seeking hope in the ghetto.
Is wealthy and gold only for the superior?
What of the deprived ,us the inferior?

Dear sky...
Was the good life made only to be watched in Hollywood movies?
Admiring Kevin Hart in those suits and ties,
What of I, the ghetto kid?
Whose drawing board is full of unfulfilled dreams
Who\'s prayer is to cry and plead

Dear sky........
For how long shall I dig deep to find gold
My hands still at hustle sweating blood.
When will I drive the truck to my destine?

Dear destine........
For you, my eyes ceased to drop tears their drop blood
My nostrils ceased to inhale oxygen but their intake poverty
Why....dear dear sky!

Dear sky......
Can you hear me......!!
Heal my wounds

Thihunaan Ibrahim Zuhair

Thihunaan is a 17 year old girl from Maldives, a small chain of islands in the Indian Ocean, who found the love for poetry at an age of 13. As far as she remembers, she always used to love reading, and a bit writing after getting inspiration from books and pieces she used to read .Especially from Wattpad. She also has an undying love for sunsets

Your handwriting

Colors fly across my eyes
As I viewed
Your handwriting from 1889
Faded ink, letters that shrunk
Oh how stupid were we
In those young lives
To think that love, and that
Ours
Would've lasted for a long time
As Written by yours , now buried hands
Aesthetically and sublime

What I regret the most

I'm glad I got passed this agony
with much more courage to embrace this grief
Almost losing all my strength
Abandoning my strongest desire
"You "
Even though i crave for your presence mightily
More than I aspired to
I was left with no choice
But to withdraw from this euphoric feeling
Of being longed for

It still hurts

I drew a line between us
Only to erase it for myself
Then I tried to draw your attention
To let myself hurt more
Was so sure I'll be fine
To see her in your arms
Guess I turn out to be the one today
Who I didn't want to be the most

Our song

Lay me on a bed of roses
To you I'd do a hundred poses
Mark, on my skin all those causes
While you embrace all my flaws's
Till you make a song
And that for us, of our own
And when you hear it
Your ears, as well ; heart bleeds
And your head gets filled
By thoughts of
Me, and me only

Toli Riba

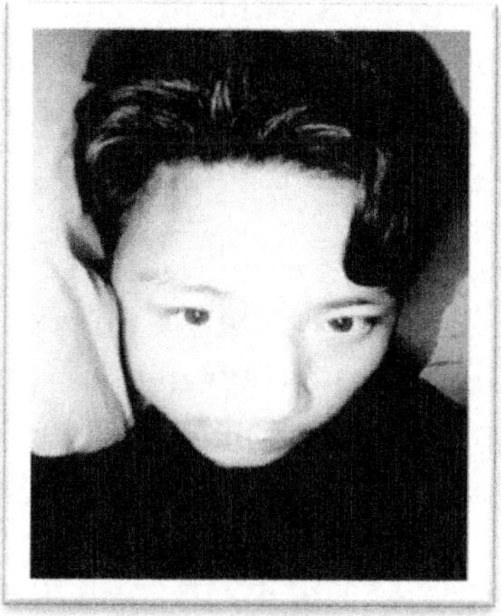

My name is Toli Riba. I am 25 years old. I hail from Arunachal Pradesh and reside in the twin city of Naharlagun. Poetry has always been very close to my heart and penning down emotions gives me a kind of gratification that no else medium of expression does. I have been writing for years but never actually had the chance to put my pages in a book. I hope you like the Poems.

Magic

You left behind, Your Hair Band
Roped like a bracelet around my Hand
And I'm taken aback to the night before
How I untied & caressed those silky waves
I said this way you look beautiful, even more

It smells of last night's magic
The exchange of two passionate physique
My skin still lingers the fragrance of you
My cigarette stained lips blush of Cherry Red
Intensity breeds in the hair strands, fallen a few

I read you Poetry as you lay bare on my Chest
Poems of Beauty, Sensuality, of Lovers & their quest
The acoustics of your Heart in your silence I heard
The depths of your soul in your eyes I saw
As you listened to the subliminal messages, The Winged Word

And it was Perfect, You were Perfect
The stars must align for such nights to exact
And as I lie in bed penning with my Heart slain
Still dosed & intoxicated, the thrill, not gone yet
I can't help but wonder, "Here I go again!"

Are You the Crowd?

I was with Youth, and I became a Rebel
I was with Excess, and I became an Addict
I was with Pleasure, and I became a Whoremonger
I was with Abuse, and I became Suicidal
I was with Dirt, and I became a Disease

This is the Power of the Crowd
From the Streets to right up in your mind, Its crowded
People follow the Crowd
Not many pave their own Path
So Are you the Crowd?

Has the Dream died?
Are you wasting away?
I see many outside who have just given up
Engulfed in the repetition of routine
From where they are to where they could have been

Or is there still a piece of you breathing a little?
Do you think about it every day?
Learn to be alone
Do not be a Lifeless face I keep seeing in the Crowd
The Crowd doesn't care about you

It steals your Identity
Bound & Defeated you come here, it kills you even further
You can breathe here, but its suffocating
You get paid here, but it's not gratifying

You have friends here, but they're not the
friendship kind

Ask me......I know all too well
I am the Crowd!

Love is its Own Language

For the Hopeless Romantics...

The Young Spaniard walks the streets of La Ville
Lumière
Paris...........
The City of Love which is
The air is scented with Le Parfum de la Romance
Lost in its Essence as he breathes the Exuberence.

His Heart spoke tender, "Compra Una Rosa!"
For a Lover is not right beside
But this Rose ignites a Light inside
"Donde estas mi Amante?" Whither are you shy?
Come! Live with me, I am but a Hopeless Romantic
guy.

There she sat, Une Belle Mademoiselle
Le Restaurant, as her fingers lay smooth on the
wind-blown hair
Shuffling through Joyce Mansour's collection, 'Les
Damnations', she looked fair
'La Vie en Rose' the ballad of Love plays aloud
The sun glistening on her skin, as the coffee steam
floats like a cloud.

"Si!" Says He, This Rose belongs to thee
In awe of her Beauty, onward to proceed
"Perdoneme ! Mujer Joven"..............."Oui!"
"Para ti !"........................"Merci Beaucoup!"

And a Kiss to make this moment, A Memory Forever.

For what are words when two Hearts engage?
Love is its own Language.

Ursula de Beer

Ursula de Beer
Date of birth: 29 September 2001
Country of birth: South Africa.
She is still a high school student, in her senior year. She started writing Poetry on the 1st January 2021. She completely fell in love with the idea of it and started to post it on social media. Things progressed from there on. She was given the opportunity to participate in a poetry anthology, and has dreams of achieving a lot of success with her writing, by releasing her own anthology someday.

I rise, I fall,

I crumble, I crawl,
But I survive it all.

I've been beat, bruised,

Played and fooled,

The world grew cold,

But I never fold,

I made it, I lost it,

But I don't regret it,

Days are good, days are bad,

I win, I lose,

But I get to choose,

Will it break me, or will it make me,

It's up to me to decide,

Will I give up and hide,

Or will I rise up and win the fight.

Do the trees get lonely?

When the seasons change
From summer,
to autumn,
The leaves come twirling down,
The trees loses a part of them.
Slowly,
day by day,
They become bare,
All alone,
by them self,
The naked branches,
They seem so dull,
Now I wonder,
Do the trees get lonely from losing part of their soul?

The Power of Addiction

Like an infant needs his mother,
So am I with you.
Fill my lungs with poison,
The thick dark clouds hang around.
My walls are stained with you,
You are slowly killing me,
How I hate you,
Still, I fail to let you go,
You are no good for me
Yet, I light you up again,
Is it me who need you
Or is it you who need me?
It is a never ending fight,
When it seemed like I defeated you,
You crawl back into my system.

Usman Mukhtar

Usman Mukhtar loves writing and traveling, he had grown up with his Nigerian parents and now a student of Bayero University Mano, Nigeria.

Trees don't have Gall

Like the tree Orange!
She has never seen PawPaw's softness annoying
they may be happy other trees live.

Ugwu grows on tress and on sticks

She burdened them to eat from her unwanted green

she is plucked to serve man's soups.

Orange lived fair

Firm she spread her wings

PawPaw's days stars have numbered

He lives after given it yellows

happy yellows like juice.

With Love Tongue

My love tongue
in a manner I have colored
The mode I communicate love
i have been talking to you!

Reply me in love language
Your ways are cashier
This time do it for yourself
You Deserve greater when you want greatness.

Walk like the two great men to become the third one.
Think like big and act like wish
Change your lenses,
kill your self-pity.

Child days are old
walk outside or stay in door
out of your comfort zone
Walk your thought out
out of all mental guard room.

Feel free the world Is a free place to do and die
The death we fear is always after us even as we run away
While I whisper words shrouded by love.

Stay strong and walk towards the mud, it's going to be thick
I will lead you but be ready to let go sweet and wit

Procrastinate now and call me later a cheat!
Going is all I have known.

If you have your love language let me know
my own language did you understand?
The words I whisper
In every way I have act?

W. Roshani M. Fernando.

Roshani Fernando is a poet, an undergraduate in B.A.(Hons)English.She is the writer @theelysianpoet, her official instagram poetry page.Further, she lives in Madampe, Srilanka, with her parents and two siblings.

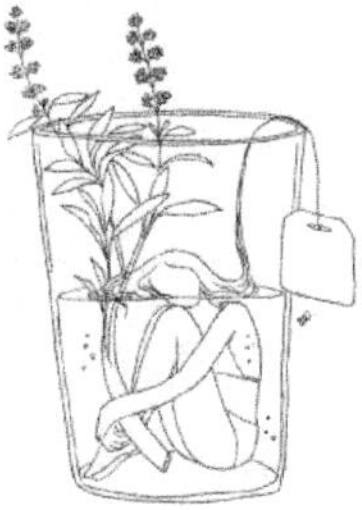

Red Velvet Macrons

They say, "Red Velvet Macrons".
Adored in red and ornamented in white.
Every single hand does move to owe her.
Her fragrance improvises sole hearts.
The elegant pace drags everyone's
attention.
Beauty is her attribute;
And Purity is her asset .
Showcased with delicacy,
For the prospective buyers
Greediness can buy her
And chomp her into pieces.
But a passionate diner will smoothly savor the
blend of her unique flavors.
In the hope to enjoy her awe-inspiring beauty,
Calmly.

Enthralling

Enthralling, her smile,
placidly springs up.
When the tender warmth
salaciously, glances at her soul.
Her cherry lips mime
a huge sigh of relief.
When a myriad of butterflies
dangling in her innermost bosom.
Her glimmering eyes lost,
in a caress void.
Her soft long fingers are gently clutched.
Redefining the promising delight.

The Chapel Bell Chimed.

The chapel bell chimed, sharp at 12.00 am.
like in fairy tales, his hand moved towards mine.
in the bliss of ma acceptance .
cheerfully, we danced along the flowery aisle.
the sweet and tendered night breeze; awoke our rusty souls.
the limbs moved to the melody of our beating hearts.
thus, old and slow, yet dazzling and precise.
it's 3.00 am in the morning,
the flourishing fragrance of white carnations,
unveiled ma inner conscience.
i tiptoed to the aroma of the incentives,
that are burning around you....
lonely, he lays in deafening silence ;
handsomely dressed in his ideal suit.
smiling in peace on a snow white fluffy blanket .
hands crossed with a rose petal scented rosary.
my weary grieving soul is in search of your beating heart.

Zaina shakeel

Zaina is a student. She loves to write her feelings and views .She loves being around the people who loves m care for her .She is fond of classical music and dance .She loves to write dark poems.

I would be Forgotten

I drift in and out of people lives
Like a feather in the breeze
You really never know I'm there
Until I start to leave
I don't make my connection deep
Because I am scared of what I will lose
I don't compete with anyone else
And I will never make you choose
I prefer to stick to sidelines
Because the spotlight hurts my eyes
I hide behind a constant smile
So you won't know it's a disguise
People tend to forget I'm there
When I'm in a crowded room
I can disappear on days on end
And I'm bound to do it soon
Don't worry if you notice I'm gone
I never meant to stay
But I know won't miss me for long
I WILL BE FORGOTTEN IN A DAY!

Zainab Ansari

Zainab was born in Uttar Pradesh. She is an avid writer. She is passionate about painting though "she loves to paint their thoughts". Her social media handle is i_zainabansari you can find her there. She usually writes in Hindi. She discovered her interest in writing when she was
in 10th standard.

Love me Anyway!!

I don't ask you to take me
Where nobody disturbs us
But I ask you to take me
Where you and your loved ones appreciate my presence.
I don't ask you to take me
Where nobody hinder us.
But I ask you to take me
Where you find a way to love me anyway.
I don't ask you to take me
To the peaceful place,
But I ask you to take me
To your home and make your home a peaceful place.
I don't claim that I love you the most
But I claim there is no one who can love you as much as the person who gave you birth.
Please don't ask me to love you,
But ask me to love your World (parents)
I don't ask you to
Always be at my side,
But I ask you to be a Man
Who can draw a line amidst righteous and wrongfulness
Who know what is fruitful.
I don't ask you to love me
The way I am
But I ask you to find a way to love me anyway.

Printed in Great Britain
by Amazon

17458509R00159